HOW TO BE A CHRISTIAN PSYCHIC

What the Bible Says about Mediums, Healers and Paranormal Investigators

ADRIAN LEE

Wisdom Editions

Minneapolis, Minnesota

Wisdom
Editions
Minneapolis

FIRST EDITION JUNE 2015
HOW TO BE A CHRISTIAN PSYCHIC: What the Bible Says about
Mediums, Healers and Paranormal Investigators.
Copyright © 2015 by Adrian Lee.
All rights reserved.

Printed in the United States of America.
10 9 8 7 6 5 4 3 2 1

Cover and interior design: Gary Lindberg

ISBN: 978-1-939548-34-4

To my Mother, whose reaction to me placing an old creepy china doll in her bed as a child still makes me laugh. The underwater video footage of her first driving test is still a constant source of awe and wonder in our family.

To my Father, the king of the unfinished project, whose philanthropic chauffeuring skills allowed me to embrace so much in my teenage years; I am sorry that I still struggle to substitute quadratic equations despite his best efforts. There are three kinds of people in this world: those that are good at math and those that aren't.

To my sister Joanne, despite not allowing me to play on your Donkey Kong game in 1979.

And finally to Heather, Lorna, Jyeton, Kathy, Nathan, Kim and Greg. Yesterday brought the beginning, tomorrow brings the end, and somewhere in the middle we became the best of friends.

Matthew 24:42

Therefore keep watch, because you do not know on what day your Lord will come.

HOW TO BE A CHRISTIAN PSYCHIC

What the Bible Says about Mediums, Healers and Paranormal Investigators

ADRIAN LEE

Notes

In this book, when I have quoted from the Bible I have remained faithful to the way it appears in print complete with antiquated spellings and quirky grammar. Every quote used within this text has come from the New International Version (NIV) Bible unless otherwise stated.

Introduction

Most people are open to the idea that there's more to life than just the physical realm; yet this understanding can be stifled or driven underground by an individual's religious beliefs—often through a misunderstanding of what the Bible tells us, or through the misplaced words of religious leaders.

Throughout our lives we all touch upon the experiences of the spirit world to a lesser or greater degree. Who doesn't have a ghost story or a psychic tale to tell? These moments occur when we unconsciously open our spiritual side to the intuitions and directions we are receiving from those that guide us on life's path: God, archangels, angels, spirit-guides, saints and deceased relatives. The truth is that you can be a psychic, you can be a healer, you can be a paranormal investigator, you can talk to the dead, you can feel and access the spirit world, and most of all *you can still be a Christian*! The psychic and spirit world is not something to fear. Acknowledging and exploring this realm will not make you a heathen or stop you from feeling God's Embrace. Your experiences of the spirit world are the work of the Lord!

If you feel your life is bereft of spiritual interaction, or that spiritual experiences are few and far between, consider the following paradigms and reflect upon your own life experiences. Psychic phenomena can be attributed to those moments in life when we feel a sense of foreboding only to discover that a loved one has been hurt or injured. Perhaps it was the sensation of a tragic event yet to unfold. Or you may have experienced your cell phone ring and instinctively knew who it was. It could be that feeling you had when looking at a new home and just knew whether it was right or wrong before you even saw beyond the hallway. You may have interacted with a spirit by smelling your deceased grandmother's perfume as you walked into her room, or your father's pipe tobacco where he used to sit. Perhaps you felt their presence close at hand just days after their passing. At such times you may have been experiencing the spiritual realm.

Ultimately, of course, it is impossible to be Christian and not believe in a spirit world. So this book seeks to be the personal model for those looking to illuminate the confusion found in the synthesis between religion and psychic phenomena. I have also witnessed a progressive polarization between two schools of thought that have not worked together—the New Age way of thinking and the traditionalist religious right. It has become very much an *us versus them* situation and neither side wants to give the other attention or facilitate any agreement that might open the door to a compromise or mutual understanding. The traditionalist approach appears to demand having everything its way with complete obedience. Those following a New Age way of thinking about Christianity feel justified in rebelling and are sick of being told what to do; they are often dismissed as diluting the word of God. What I aim to achieve in this book is the middle ground. I straddle both worlds as an analytical thinker with experience of the Divine. This allows me to identify the facts and look at the evidence—to hopefully embrace all and allow a middle ground to be created in this polemic model.

For me, nearly half a lifetime passed before I realized that many random acts of life weren't random at all. Even the dark things that happened to me turned out to be beautiful. In hindsight I realized that I had needed them, without understanding it at the time. This marked the beginning of wisdom in my life. I often found myself falling into the convention of saying *that was a strange coincidence,* or *I can't believe that just happened.* This was a difficult paradigm to break out of and it took me years to do so.

As an art historian, my specialty is the early Italian Renaissance period. During my studies I have often wondered why I had become so curiously drawn to this era of art history. It might have been that my analytical mind was intrigued with the struggle of artists in that period to create depth on a flat two-dimensional surface using geometrical illusions such as vanishing points and horizons. Or I may have been fascinated by their attempts with chemical experiments to create the earliest paints using ground-up semi-precious stones and egg yolks. It also may have been my interest in their naïve endeavor to understand anatomy and how the body worked, and the artist's tortured battles to make the fingers look as realistic as possible as Mary clutched the baby Jesus to her chest.

Of course, it could have been simply the awe and wonder of walking out of the blazing bright sun of a Tuscan summer into the cool, dark sanctuary of a fourteenth-century chapel where I was captivated by the sparkling, gold-embossed frescos that scattered light from a smoky candle around the sainted images. Only now do I believe that more was taking place in me beneath this veneer of my cultural preoccupations.

In those moments of study and my endless beautiful trips to the terracotta-dripped vistas of northwestern Italy, I was slowly gaining a substantial knowledge of the Bible, almost through osmosis. I did not know it at the time, but as I picked my way through the olive-tree-lined countryside I was becoming immersed and informed of the Bible and its stories. This, in many respects, is a tribute to those early Italian masters that rose above the ranks of common artisan to create a whole new genre and profession—that of the *artist*. With a clutch of church money, these pioneering individuals depicted the stories of the Bible on the sacred holy walls using a mixture of chemistry, inspiration, skill and alacrity. Originally their task was to provide visual imagery to educate the illiterate masses about the power and light of the gospel. The result was a giant formalist comic-book-like narrative. Nearly six hundred years later, as I stood in front of these images holding my dictionary of Biblical characters and places, they once again informed in the same way they had when the plaster was still drying. My visually wired brain was remembering everything and I soaking in all the information that was presented.

Despite my fascination with the paranormal as an adult, I spent my childhood without any discernible spiritual interest. I fidgeted in endless lectures delivered by apathetic religious teachers in visually redundant chalk-dust-covered classrooms in a school for the terminally frustrated and partially interested. But now I was finding knowledge inspirationally implanted by the very method Masaccio, Masolino, Giotto, Cimabue and Duccio had strived to induce all those centuries ago into the local congregation. Of course, I was unaware that my path was being predetermined as I sought to enjoy the fine pastas, seductive wines and sandy beaches.

Many years later, it was a big leap geographically and polemically when I found myself tentatively making my way through the dank unwelcoming passages of a haunted basement in Minnesota during a bitterly cold January. But in that nineteenth-century river-rock-constructed basement I encountered my first demonic entity. I was not looking for such phenomena. I was happy wandering around in the ignorance of such beings as I strove to improve my understanding of history by investigating ghosts and talking to the dead. But as the basement's darkness shrouded me like a thick army blanket, and the smell of sulfur issued into the air to combine with the animal-like noises of snuffling and scratching, I wondered what armor I had. What was my protection, and what and where were my tools to survive or defeat such mysterious entities?

My vulnerability was brought into sharp focus when I witnessed a team member scratched from head to toe in talon-shaped gouges. At that moment, if I had to acknowledge through violent fact that Biblical evil exists, then by default I had to acknowledge that Biblical good must *also* exist. It was then I decided to follow the path to God as I sought to bring the light of the Gospel into my life. It seemed ironic that it was my exposure to Biblical evil that pushed me into God's embrace. There was no angelic message or divine vision for me. That would come much later. Instead, I experienced the stench and filth of crawling around an insalubrious basement with evil lurking about.

My new commitment to gain knowledge and understanding of the Bible came from a position of ignorance. I had never been to church, other than for the odd funeral and a few weddings, so I started to study theology. I attended several Christian camps, befriended a few pastors, and interacted with religious leaders—even some who called themselves prophets. Over time I realized that my knowledge had become surprisingly advanced and I was able to see how the Bible stories and characters artistically depicted in Italy related to my newfound understanding.

I was aware of the story of Jesus and the Tribute Money as told in Matthew 17:24, because Masaccio had painted it on the wall of the Brancacci Chapel in the Santa Maria del Carmine in Florence during the 1420s. I knew of the Supper at Emmaus, Luke 24:13-35, because I had stood gazing at the painting for many hours admiring the chiaroscuro and symbolism within Caravaggio's work. I knew St. Stephen had been stoned to death, Acts 7:54-60, because Jacopo di Cioni had depicted him balancing a stone on his head in one of twelve paneled altar pieces commissioned for the San Pier Maggiore in 1370.

It was then that my studies of the Bible grew into a concern because what was preached from the altar was not my experience of the afterlife and the psychic world. I had seen the darkest entities, I had spoken and interviewed the dead, and I was able to have an awareness of the future, yet I encountered many individuals who claimed to be speaking on behalf of God while denouncing and denigrating my psychic investigations and experiences. These clerics, I had to remind myself, had no right to claim they were spiritually enlightened while demonstrating such personal vindictiveness. The conventional religious thinking among the clergy and many congregants was false. Over time, many untruths had become known as facts. But I had evidence to back up my beliefs.

Messages I had actually read in the Bible, the true word of God, contradicted many church teachings. And so I knew someone had to set the record straight. And that someone would have to be me. It is the modern way that an accuser needs no evidence to make accusations, but the accused must produce evidence to defend himself. This, then, is the genesis of this book, which highlights the events throughout my life that led me to this very point, *How to be a Christian Psychic: what the Bible says about Mediums, Healers and Paranormal Investigators*.

Let me make one caveat, however. Even though we have the Bible as the written word of God, none of us knows the Mind of God. So none of us should speak on His behalf or claim otherwise—including me. This is highlighted in the passages below.

Isaiah 55:8
"For my thoughts are not your thoughts, neither are your ways my ways," declares the LORD.

1 Corinthians 2:11
For who knows a person's thoughts except their own spirit within them? In the same way no one knows the thoughts of God except the Spirit of God.

This book, then, relies for its fundamental arguments solely on the words written and documented in the Bible.

2 Timothy 3:16
All Scripture is God-breathed and is useful for teaching, rebuking, correcting and training in righteousness...

During the process of revisiting the Biblical text, I wanted to understand why my vocation as a psychic, healer and paranormal investigator was so offensive to some members of the Christian church despite the Bible's admonitions to use our God-given gifts to help others. I was also concerned that my fellow Christian psychics and healers might be going through similar attacks and rejections.

I believed it would be a profound loss to the service of humankind if they repressed their gifts because of uninformed pressure by the church and community.

Although this book will be a stark rebuke to those who wish to suppress the practices of psychics, I do not wish to judge. God knows every hair on our heads. And He is, of course, the ultimate judge. I only want to present the evidence I have found to support my ideas. Undoubtedly, some will accuse me of cherry-picking parts of the Bible to make my arguments. I guess this is true, in that I have used some passages of the Bible as evidence to make a point or cause some understanding to occur just as any historian would do. The fact remains that these passages are in the Bible for all to see. And I might point out that dissenters from my point-of-view will likely cherry-pick their own parts of the Bible to support their own arguments.

What I discovered throughout my research was that those individuals who condemn psychics for not following the word of God are not adhering to the actual Biblical text themselves. Hypocrisy and religion seem to go hand-in-hand, unfortunately. For example, a person attempting to obey every part of Leviticus would quite rightly be sent to prison. It would be impossible to remain true to this Old Testament design for life, especially if one wished to stay firmly within the framework of modern society. And yet, those who attack psychics selectively use the words of Leviticus to support their convictions. But the words are taken out of context. The following statements, for example, are found in Leviticus.

Leviticus 19:31
Do not turn to mediums or seek out spiritists, for you will be defiled by them. I am the LORD YOUR GOD.

Leviticus 20:6
"I will set my face against anyone who turns to mediums and spiritists to prostitute themselves by following them, and I will cut them off from their people."

There are two ways to address the text of the Lord in reference to the Old Testament. There is a fundamentalist approach that takes every word at face value. These Christians believe there was actually a real Garden of Eden, that Noah really existed, and that all of the Bible stories are historical documentations of real events and people. It would be easy to respond to this fundamentalist approach to attacking the psychic or healer by using a fundamentalist approach—if you bring a sword, I will also go and get a sword. But the bigger picture must be explored. If I choose to respond with a fundamentalist approach to the Leviticus quotes above, I would have to use the other parts of the text word for word also. This puts into perspective the concept of *cherry picking* because within the same nineteenth chapter of Leviticus the Bible says the following:

Leviticus 19

[19] Do not wear clothing woven of two kinds of material.

[26] Do not eat any meat with the blood still in it.

[27] Do not cut the hair at the sides of your head or clip off the edges of your beard.

[28] Do not cut your bodies for the dead or put tattoo marks on yourselves. I am the LORD.

I am currently writing this paragraph in a yellow poly-cotton shirt with a trimmed beard and two tattoos. I prefer my steak medium rare, if anyone is asking. Do these behaviors make me in any way less righteous or further from God? I find it hard to believe that my loving and forgiving God would punish me (when I seek to practice good things through his Christian ideologies) because I have a closet full of polo shirts. This logic places the previous condemning statements of Leviticus into the perspective of the time in which they were written. It now seems ridiculous that these ordinances could be applied derogatorily toward a psychic today.

There is also a second approach to understanding the Leviticus passages. This is to understand the Bible in terms of a constructed text taken from folklore, memories of historical incidents, and superstitious traditions. This approach proposes that the Old Testament stories are a collection of metaphors and parables (arguably the first recorded historical fusion of known wisdom) bundled together in one volume to enable us to understand the essence of what God requires of us.

A response from this second approach would require a deeper knowledge and awareness of how and why the Leviticus text was written and composed. We can gain such awareness by remembering the period of history in which these specific rules would have been enforced and reasons why they may have been necessary then—for example, to keep people alive and healthy. These laws were introduced in a context way outside of western 21st century living. The main theme of Leviticus is that a faithful enactment of ritual will make God's presence available, thus the breaking or ignoring of these rules compromises the harmony between God and man *during this period*. These rules were given to the Hebrew people for the correction and conduct of their OWN people. For Christians, it should be viewed as a document of that previous time, not of our time.

I will soon respond fully to those individual statements from Leviticus that solely attack the medium and spiritualist. But first, I want to help you understand the context of these writings and how some individuals selectively use the written word out of its context to create conflicts.

It is important to remember, however, that contradictions also abound within the Bible. A second book using the Bible as its primary source could easily present the counter argument. Here are two examples of such contradictions.

Exodus 15:3
The Lord is a warrior; the Lord is his name.

Romans 15:33
The God of peace be with you all. Amen.

Based on these passages, is the Lord a warrior or a God of peace?

Matthew 27:28
They stripped him and put a scarlet robe on him.

John 19:2
The soldiers twisted together a crown of thorns and put it on his head. They clothed him in a purple robe.

According to the Bible, what was the color of Christ's robe?

What is required in this text is not just a responsibility to highlight Bible passages that indicate where the work of the psychic and healer are encouraged, but to also analyze passages that attack and denounce the idea of these practices. In this way perhaps we can gain a deeper understanding of why such passages have been written and what their true meaning may be. As a methodology, this would be based on Hegelian theory developed by the German Philosopher Georg Wilhelm Friedrich Hegel at the beginning of the 19th century. Hegel stated that when you write a thesis (book), in due course another author will write an anti-thesis (a book in response to the first book). Then a third author will eventually write a synthesis combining the ideas from the first two texts, thus creating a whole new book. The process will then start all over again. My task is to make the second book (the anti-thesis) as difficult to write as possible.

During the course of my research I have realized that some individuals were unsure or worried about the concept of a spiritual world that cannot be easily seen or explained by science. The truth is, some things are beyond science, beyond what anyone knows. This could be described as needing to have faith. Remember that some people cannot see the color red, but the color red still exists. I am also aware that people are deterred from embracing the psychic and spiritual world by the words that are used to describe these phenomena. The words "paranormal," "metaphysical" and "supernatural" have negative connotations placed upon them and can evoke an emotive response.

Let me break down these words in an etymological context and dispel any myth or preconceived thinking that has been placed upon their usage. The term "paranormal" has been in use since the early 1920s. It derives from the combination of the word "para," which reflects *above*, *beyond*, or *contrary to*; and the word "normal," the definition of which implies that scientific reasoning is within a normal range of experience or explanation.

The term "supernatural" derives from the Medieval Latin *supernātūrālis,* meaning above nature. The word was recorded as far back as the 1520s and describes subjects that are beyond, or cannot be explained by, the laws of physics—things that exist above and beyond nature.

The term "metaphysical" derives from the Greek word metá, meaning beyond, upon, or after, and the word *physiká*. It was first used as the title for several of Aristotle's works, which were usually anthologized after the works on physics in complete editions. The prefix *meta-* (beyond) simply indicates that these works come *after* the chapters on physics.

So all three words have their origins in describing an event that cannot be explained by scientific theory. Yet nearly every narrative in the Bible would be unexplainable by scientific theory—from Eve being created from one of Adam's ribs, to Jesus' acts of walking on water and turning water into wine. As we know, science is usually late to the party, typically explaining things we already knew were in place. For example, quantum physics is only now just starting to understand that a collective consciousness in the universe can be proven by the act of micro-waves being held in stasis by event horizons created by black holes. This theory is currently being explored by the Harvard professor Rudy Schild and many others.

I also wish to state that just because science cannot prove something, does not mean it does not exist. Before 1992, we believed that the universe only contained nine planets. We have now discovered over 1,000 planets thanks to the Hubble space telescope and Kepler space observatory. This does not mean that before 1992 those unknown planets did not exist—we just did not know about them then. Of course the Americas still existed before they were found by Western European explorers, and electricity existed before it was understood and harnessed.

Preface

I want to use the preface to illustrate why this book is so important to me, as I believe that my own personal experiences of the Divine and spiritual world have shaped my thinking and beliefs. These true events informed my thoughts and placed me on the path I am now on. I want to share the details of those interactions to illustrate fully the power of the gospel and the strength of prayer. It was the darkness that I saw in a Minnesotan basement that propelled me towards God. Subsequently, I saw more of the light of goodness on my continuing journey.

Angel Visitation: Morning of May 12, 2011

Several days before my angelic experience, I asked God a very interesting question in a prayer. I was slowly beginning to be drawn into the idea of writing a book about the history of angels—their symbolism and meaning, and how they are portrayed in art and literature (still an ongoing project as I write this book). I knew this was going to be a huge undertaking with many years of hard study, and I did not know if I was ready to commit myself to such a demanding project. I asked God if this was a task I needed to undertake. *Show me an angel*, I said.

What could be a clearer sign for a book about angels?

I went to bed late on the night of Wednesday, May 11. There was an unseasonable chill in the air, and I gathered the bed covers around me for warmth. A cold cup of tea sat on my bedside cabinet untouched for thirty minutes. At the beginning of the week I had bought a small travel Bible from a secondhand bookstore in Alexandria, Minnesota, and it had become my bedtime reading. I had often looked at the towering stack of old family Bibles left in the darkest corner of the bookstore. These books needed love and a good home. They had once been treasured possessions, but people die and their Bibles find their way into dusty shops. I decided to choose one and give it a new home. This was the book at my bedside.

I had been working my way through Matthew and had been reading for around twenty minutes that particular evening before turning off my bedside lamp and going to sleep. I recall dreaming throughout the night, but no dreams stuck in my mind; but it was odd for me to be dreaming so early in the night. Most of my dreams come just before I wake up in the morning.

Near daybreak, I awoke on my left side all curled up and fumbled to move the pillow back under my head. Suddenly I became aware of the most brilliant, blinding light raining down on me from above. It was very powerful and filled the room, glowing and dazzling like the white light in the hottest part of a furnace. It was so intense that I immediately realized I could not see any of the walls or corners of the room. The ceiling had disappeared in the harsh light pouring down into the room, as if somebody had removed the ceiling and positioned a stadium floodlight over the bed.

With the light came a great heat. I kept my head to the left side because I did not want to be blinded, and I felt the heat on the exposed half of my face. It was the kind of feeling you may have experienced standing too close to a bonfire where one side of your face is cold and the other is hot. I decided to place my hand over my face to feel how hot it actually was, and this act gave my cheek some protection. I did not know what would happen next, or whether my face would become intolerably hot.

As I lay there, I knew immediately that this was a spiritual experience. I knew that from the moment it started. I did not feel afraid or scared, but rather had a feeling of benevolence. I had the empathic experience of somebody putting his hand on my shoulder and saying, *I am here*, like a close friend saying, *you know where I am; if you need me, just call.* I had the sense of being looked after and looked over.

I already had an awareness that angels can communicate via God with man through thoughts and in spirit.

Psalms 103:20
Praise the Lord, you his angels, you mighty ones who do his bidding, who obey his word.

Matthew 2:13
When they had gone, an angel of the Lord appeared to Joseph in a dream.

Hebrews 1:14
Are not all angels ministering spirits sent to serve those who will inherit salvation?

I never looked directly into the light. I felt it would be inappropriate to gaze into the glare. Its brilliance suggested that it would be impossible to see anything through the intense brightness (one does not stare directly into the sun). I also felt humbled and that I was unworthy to look, so I kept my head turned to the left side. I could see the light illuminating the bedroom door and flooding down the walls. The light also lit up the gold thread on my quilt, which eerily glowed.

I lay there calmly; I did not want the experience to disappear by making any sudden movements or commotion. There was no message and no sense of being informed of anything. I was prepared to receive a message, but none was conveyed to me—other than a Divine arm being placed around me. I believed that everything happening to me was good. It was perhaps enough to believe I would find my own message in this experience.

I then recall the light leaving as quickly as it appeared, leaving behind a dark stillness. It is hard to say how long this episode lasted, but I would guess a few minutes. When it was over, I quickly fell back to sleep, in the same way as if I had been awakened suddenly by a dog barking or a passing car.

At this point in my life I did not need proof for the existence of the Divine. I had no burning desire to have a sign of the magnitude of this experience. Don't get me wrong—I am grateful for being touched by God in this way, but a sign to prove the existence of the spirit realm was not necessary for me.

I have considered many times whether this may have been a dream. If it was, then it was unlike any dream I have ever experienced, with more detail, sound, and physicality than anything I have ever known. It was so defining that I instantly recalled the event as I woke up that morning.

My first thought was to actually glance up to see if there had been any damage to the ceiling from the nights' event. There was none. I then made my way to the bathroom. I looked in the mirror and discovered that there was a redness on the right side of my face which had been exposed to the light. To me, this was physical proof that I had not been dreaming. I went to my Bible and started to look for similar incidents, some kind of reference point or confirmation of my experience. I found the following passages:

Acts 9:3-6
As he neared Damascus on his journey, suddenly a light from heaven flashed around him. [4] He fell to the ground and heard a voice say to him, "Saul, Saul, why do you persecute me?"

[5] "Who are you, Lord?" Saul asked. "I am Jesus, whom you are persecuting," he replied.

[6] "Now get up and go into the city, and you will be told what you must do."

Luke 2:8-10
And there were shepherds living out in the fields nearby, keeping watch over their flocks at night. [9] An angel of the Lord

appeared to them, and the glory of the Lord shone around them, and they were terrified. [10] But the angel said to them, "Do not be afraid."

I then spent several days pondering the encounter I had witnessed. Was it fanciful thinking to believe that I had experienced the same type of visitation that Saul or the shepherds had received? I then walked into the guest bedroom of my house. I rarely frequent this area so it was one of the neatest in my home. I had walked in to retrieve some clothes that were stored in the closet. There on the cream-colored carpet in the middle of the floor was a shiny gold coin about the size of a quarter. I bent down and picked it up. I had never seen a coin like this before—clearly it wasn't mine. On both sides of the coin was the embossed image of an angel with its wings spread.

I have no clue how it came to be there. There were no numbers or words on the coin and no other markings. Due to its prominent display on the floor, it would have been instantly seen by any individual who entered that room, yet the coin had not been there the last time I had entered during the previous week. And nobody else had been in the house, let alone the room, for an even longer period of time. Considering the coin a lucky talisman, I placed it in my wallet. It is still there today. For me this was a reinforcement of the angel visitation I had received.

Meeting with Joshua: Evening of August 14, 2012

I was given the present of a crucifix pendant by a close friend who had found the object at a garage sale the previous week. It was made of a dull metal like tarnished pewter and looked old with its depiction of Christ on the cross. It was the kind of object I am usually drawn to because of my love of antiques, religion and the unique. The crucifix required a chain so I kept the pendant in my wallet next to my angel coin until I could find a way to wear it. And there it stayed for a week. I even forgot about its presence.

This religious Christian icon was given to me during a time when I believed quite reasonably that dark high magic was being practiced against me, and that malicious demonic entities had been placed in my path. I was struggling against these foes and frequent reinforcements of my religious convictions were important to bolster my faith.

Then, one evening about a week later, I found myself sitting alone at the kitchen dining table with my obligatory cup of tea. I suddenly felt the presence of somebody entering the room to my left. I turned my head at a right angle to see who or what was there. To my astonishment, I saw a figure just seven feet away looking directly at me! What I saw made me glance away sharply.

The reason I turned was that the figure was in a full state of decay, as if someone had just pried the lid off a coffin to reveal its grizzly contents. But ultimately, curiosity compelled me to look back. Two dark sockets were visible where eyes had once been, and the jaw was starting to dislocate and fall away to one side like a maniacal laugh. The flesh was rotting around an emaciated body, and I could see bone and skeleton in the places where the tissue had long since disappeared.

The figure's wild hair was textured with bits of skin that had become matted and had fallen away from the scalp, revealing white flashes of the skull beneath. I was nauseated by the stench of death and decay. I tried not to look at the figure, not out of a sense of terror, but more out of a feeling of respect for the person I was seeing in such a form. This was the only time I had ever seen a ghost in a state of decay.

As I sat there motionless, now staring at the refrigerator door, I could see in my peripheral view the figure walking behind me. He ended up looking directly over my shoulder to my right-hand side. I never for one moment felt a sense of foreboding or maliciousness. I had the impression that the figure had a purpose that he was trying to communicate to me. I asked who he was and he replied, *Joshua*. This was the only verbal message I received during the entire encounter.

I became tense as the figure reached out its skeletal hand to grab my right hand, which was placed palm down on the table. He gripped my hand and turned it over. The back of my hand was now in contact with the surface of the table. I loosely opened my fingers so my palm was visible, and the figure placed an object into my hand. I strained to see what I was being given but could not see it. So I asked him to do it again, and he did. Once more he placed something in my palm and once more I failed to see what I was meant to receive. This continued several more times, and on each frustrating occasion I could not see the object.

Finally, I got to see what I was being given. It was the pewter crucifix I had received the previous week and had forgotten about. I saw the image of the cross as the figure closed my hand, so I was now clutching the object. He wrapped his hand around mine to let me know that he wanted me to have it. And then he was gone. I believe this action was to reinforce how important this symbol was and to remind me it was in my possession.

I believe that Joshua, who in Biblical times led the Israelites into Canaan, had tried to show me the path I needed to take against my turmoil as he had once done with the Israelites. It was through my faith that these dark entities would be conquered. After this encounter my analytical mind spent several hours trying to convince my brain that the incident had not taken place, that I had imagined the whole thing. Why did I think I was so special that I would receive a visit from Joshua, and why did he arrive in such a state of decay?

After much thought and consideration I came to realize that Joshua had visited me because I am one of God's children, and as such I will be looked after and protected. This alone would explain why I had received a visitation from such an iconoclastic figure. I then wondered if the state of decay was actually an illusion cast upon my vision by dark entities who wanted me to react in a state of revulsion, hoping that I would flee from the message out of fear and dread. Is it possible that Joshua had actually appeared in the form of a healthy normal person, but through an evil-distorted veil was transformed into that decaying figure?

I believe Joshua was telling me that I needed to further embrace my faith and press myself into God, especially against the wall of darkness I found myself battling. Malicious, demonic forces would not want me engaging with Joshua to receive encouragement and guidance.

It was then I turned to my favorite gospel in the Bible and almost immediately found the meaning behind the vision. It was the very message I needed to receive at that specific moment in time.

2 Corinthians 4:16
Wherefore we faint not; but though our outward man is decaying, yet our inward man is renewed day by day.

Joshua's message was clear: despite physical and outward decay, we are all inwardly renewing.

At that moment I understood that I needed to remove the crucifix from its temporary home in my wallet and hang it prominently around my neck, allowing it to be the focus of my protection. I went to find a silver chain I had stored at the back of my bedside cabinet. It fit the pendant perfectly.

The next morning I went to place the crucifix back around my neck and one of the links—not a weak spot like the clasp—just broke in two. I had never witnessed such a thing before. I started to question whether the forces of darkness were intent on looking to hamper my wearing of this symbol. So I resigned myself to finding another chain.

That afternoon I was looking through the clothing in a thrift shop when I noticed an ornamental jewelry tree on the cashier's desk. I could see numerous chains displayed on it. I looked through them, and to my surprise saw the perfect silver chain for my crucifix. I placed the chain on the surface next to the till and told the cashier I would be back to pay for it but needed to go and look at a summer shirt that had caught my eye. I came back with the shirt not more than a minute later and looked for the chain, but it was gone. I asked the cashier what she had done with it, and she replied that no one had touched it. We were the only two in the shop. The two of us looked high and low for at least ten minutes, but the chain had disappeared into thin air.

I reluctantly left with just a shirt in my hand. This was now looking like a conspiracy. I was becoming single-mindedly obsessed in my mission to wear that crucifix and to gain the requisite chain. I jumped in the car and found myself in a small secondhand jewelry store that I had driven by on many occasions. I entered and saw a large array of jewelry. A middle-aged, bearded gentleman greeted me and asked if he could help. I responded that I was looking for a silver chain.

"I always have a lot of chains. I buy them and then don't sell them. Let me have a look," he replied, then proceeded to show me a bag full of gold chains.

"What kind of gold chain would you like?" he asked.

"No, I need a silver chain," I replied.

"I don't sell many, but let me have a look."

He came back after a short while with a further selection of gold chains.

"Sorry, I asked for silver chains," I said, frustrated.

"Would you like to see some gold rings? I have a lot of gold rings."

"No, thank you—I want a silver chain," I replied once again.

It was if he had become ignorant of the word silver and could not make out the request I was making. He seemed slightly baffled as to what I was actually asking for, and the whole scene had a macabre spell of miscommunication and misunderstanding about it. No matter how many times I told him I wanted a silver chain, he could not understand or process the information, so finally I just left. I knew I had a natural leather tie at home, so I decided not to fight any dark forces over the silver chain.

In my experiences working with clients I have found dark forces will do everything in their powers to remove you from the paths you need to go down, the paths that will bring you success and happiness as guided by God. I have on many occasions found myself driving to a client's house to remove dark and evil energies and entities. Those beings are fully aware that I am coming to take them away and destroy them. When going on such a mission, I have experienced:

- Suddenly being overtaken with an overwhelming tired-ness, one that forces me to pull the vehicle over into a rest area.

- A sudden and unexpected thunderstorm that made driving conditions hazardous.

- A flat tire or other car-related breakdown or mishap.

- A hornet flying through the open car window and down my shirt.

- The strange feeling of being blind to the road I needed when making my way to a location, and unable to see it on a map, as if it had been erased from my vision like a temporary dyslexia.

In every circumstance though, I have persevered and made my way successfully to the client's house, and taken care of what need-ed to be done.

It is my experience that if you heal or perform psychic work in the name of the Lord, then those that fear, those that despise, those that hate to see you use that process, will attack you and want to see you fail. They will project their thoughts into others, who will then ridicule and ostracize you even from within your own church and community. I say, in the face of such actions: *is that the best that you can do?* I don't say this to goad them, but to inform them and their puppet masters that my faith and strength is greater than theirs, and that I cannot be taken away from the Divine path by their antics. I have issued this question over and over whenever I find my path blocked. God and having faith in God will overthrow and conquer all that the opposition has to throw. This has given me the power to remain strong and unrelenting.

Postscript

It was not until some considerable time after my encounter with Joshua that I realized I may have misjudged the entire incident. I became aware through research that the early first century writings documenting Jesus and His life had failed to use His name correctly. In His day, Jesus was actually known as Joshua ben Joseph.

First century accounts of Jesus were written in Greek using the term Iησους (*Iesous*), which translates back to the Hebrew name Joshua (meaning *Yahweh is salvation*). We get the English name Jesus from the Latin translation of the Greek manuscripts by Jerome in the early fifth century. The typical Jewish naming convention *Jesus (Joshua) son of Joseph* is actually used in Luke 4:22 and in John, but the Greek-speaking gentiles preferred titles with theological implications and moved quickly towards *Jesus Christ* or *Christ Jesus*. Since Jesus and Joseph were common names in the first century, early Christians sought to differentiate their Jesus by using *Jesus of Nazareth*, *Jesus, son of David*, and of course *Jesus, Son of God*.

As you are now aware, this puts a whole new perspective on my encounter. It also brings uncertainty as to who my ghostly visitor actually was. Regardless of identity (Joshua or Jesus) the message remains the same and very clear, and I am grateful beyond words to have been touched in such a profoundly Divine way.

This book is a culmination of these Divine visits and experiences combined with my education and knowledge gained as a historian and theologian. With my extensive background in paranormal investigating, mixed with my successful career as a psychic and healer, I have been given a unique set of tools by our Lord to be able to undertake this book, and here is the result.

Mark 1:15

"The time has come," he said. "The kingdom of God has come near. Repent and believe the good news!"

The Hidden Context of the Bible

Before we start to analyze the Biblical text further, it is important to understand the primary source material we are working with— how the Bible came about and the meta-narratives that are woven throughout the text. If we are to quote the Good Book, then we need to understand why it was written and who it was written for.

The Bible is derived from so many sources and translations that clarity in these matters is an almost impossible task; one could easily write a book on this topic by simply picking a random Biblical passage and studying it. Given its complexity and multiple sources, I still find it remarkable that I can use the text of the Bible to find an argument to back up my beliefs, considering the dark agenda that surrounded the translations in the King James Bible, a version that has provided character of Christian thought and belief for the last four hundred years. So let us start by looking at the earliest influences on the Biblical text and Christian thinking.

Christianity as a formal religion originated in the first-century Roman province of Judea, a predominantly Jewish society with traditional Judaist philosophies. The origin here was primarily due to the life and teachings of Jesus. Because of Christianity's development from within the Jewish faith, the religion was established free from most pagan beliefs and customs and distinct from the Greek thought that was dominant throughout the Roman Empire during this era. Tensions between these two ideologies and the early Christian church were highlighted by Paul in his writings against the Greek philosophy in 1st Corinthians. He drew our attention to these profoundly different ways of thinking when he discussed the encounters he'd had with Epicurean and Stoic philosophers in Acts. He then proceeded to warn against philosophical vanities in the text of Colossians 2:8.

Christianity first came into contact with pagan ideologies and teachings due to its rapid spread via successful missionary work into the sprawling Roman Empire. Many freshly converted Christians still held onto some of their past pagan ways, but from within the newly implanted Christian framework. Anglo-Saxon conversion was one of the most difficult conversions to obtain for Christian missionaries because paganism was so entrenched into their culture. The Saxons were one of the last groups to be converted, mainly due to the threat of death under Charlemagne's rule and later concessions made by Christian missionaries. Some of these concessions included elements of pagan worship.

A letter written in June A.D. 601 by Pope Gregory to Mellitus (the first bishop of London) actually documents the appropriation of pagan festivals and temples into Christian use.

> *The temples of the idols in that nation ought not to be destroyed; but let the idols that are in them be destroyed; let holy water be made and sprinkled in the said temples, let altars be erected, and relics placed. For if those temples are well built, it is requisite that they be converted from the worship of devils to the service of the true God...*

Anglo-Saxon conversion in particular was a gradual process that included many compromises and syncretism, or the fusing together of two or more forms of belief. The letter also alludes to this methodology: *he who endeavours to ascend to the highest place rises by degrees or steps, and not by leaps.*

During the early Middle Ages, the Christianization of Europe adopted many of the rituals and traditional elements of folk religion.

Pagan festivals and ceremonies were embraced by the Christian church and made into modern holidays. For example, the pagan celebration of the Vernal Equinox was Christianized and presented as the Annunciation to the Blessed Virgin Mary, celebrated as the Feast of the Annunciation. The Summer Solstice was also renamed and represented as the Christian holiday associated with the nativity of John the Baptist and observed on June 24. Other central concepts surrounding modern Christianity—such as altars, candles, robes, incense, Christmas, and even the cross—all have European pagan roots. This seemed to be the perfect synthesis of Christian doctrine intermixed with pagan festivals and rituals as prescribed and encouraged by the Pope.

It was at the beginning of the 17th century that the Biblical text was used as a tool to attack and admonish the work of psychics, spiritualists and healers. The King James English translations of the Christian Bible for the Church of England was begun in 1604 and completed in 1611. King James oversaw the translations personally to guarantee that the new book would conform to the ecclesiology and Episcopal framework of the Church of England and its belief in ordained clergy. The king issued his own instructions for how he wanted the new translation to be constructed. King James believed that previous translations of the Bible were imperfect. The Bishop's Bible and scriptures were considered to be too lazy in their translations, and the Puritan's Geneva Bible had been written by protestant scholars with an anti-monarchist bias.

King James' mother Mary was strongly Roman Catholic at a time when most people and parliament were fiercely protestant. This was a unique period in history during which the compass of religion was held at the very center of power and society, and when people believed religious faith was not only worth living for, but dying for as well. Society wanted the truth about God and the way of salvation. They wanted a resolution to the corruption of His church on earth—a Presbyterian unity.

This, then, set the scene for young King James who had just returned from Oslo in the spring of 1590 after marrying Anne, the daughter of the King of Denmark-Norway. The Danish court at that time was greatly concerned with the threat of witchcraft and the black arts, and this must have impressed the king. Subsequently, the royal voyage back from Denmark was beset with storms. This was perceived to be the work of witchcraft and instigated a witch hunt in Copenhagen that summer. One of the first victims, under duress, divulged the names of five other women who all then confessed to practicing sorcery to raise storms to menace Queen Anne's voyage. The women claimed they had sent devils to climb the keel of her ship. In September of that year, two of the women were burned in Kronborg.

The Witchcraft Act was implemented in 1563 in Britain, but the first major prosecution under this new law came in 1590 when James set up his own tribunal after hearing the news from Denmark. He took a personal involvement in the proceedings and personally supervised the torture of women accused of witchcraft in what became known as the North Berwick witch trials. One of the courts' victims was a healer and midwife by the name of Agnes Sampson. Sampson admitted to practicing witchcraft in a confession given under torture. She was then taken to Castle Rock in Edinburgh where she was garroted and burned at the stake.

King James' growing obsession with witches led him to write his 1597 book *Daemonologie*, a text attacking the practice of witchcraft which inspired the Shakespeare tragedy *Macbeth*. In this book, King James supports the practice of witch hunting.

King James used his own translation of the Bible to reinforce his own convictions. It is important to understand that King James grouped psychics, mediums, witches, plague spreaders, demon summoners, sorcerers and spiritualists all together into one heretical group. He believed that if you heal, see the future, talk to the dead or have premonitions, you must be doing it with the allegiance and help of Satan. These beliefs stirred up a terrified population in the wake of the Black Death of 1348-1350.

Adding to this growing fear of heretics was the text *Malleus Maleficarum* (*Hammer of the Witches*). This book was a treatise on the prosecution of witches published in 1487 and written by a German Catholic clergyman named Heinrich Kramer. The late 1400s was an earlier period of religious turmoil that witnessed increasing intolerance of the Reformation and Counter-Reformation. Between 1487 and 1520, the work was published thirteen times; it was published another sixteen times between 1574 and 1669. One could argue that due to the development of mechanized printing, this was the first international bestselling book.

This, then, is the context, background, influence and thinking of the man who implemented, translated, funded, printed and distributed what is arguably the most successful and influential book of all time—the King James Bible. So let us now apply this knowledge to the text his influence and beliefs produced. The phrase below is taken from Exodus and is often quoted by fundamentalist Christians to suppress and denigrate the work of anyone in the psychic field. Remember that the term *witch* was applied to all manner of practices.

Exodus 22:18
Thou shalt not suffer a witch to live.

The King James text, like most other translations of the period, was translated from Hebrew and Aramaic texts that had been translated into Greek and Latin, and then into English. As anyone who knows a foreign language will tell you, some concepts and words simply do not cross over well from one language to another. Translation can be inadvertently tainted or even deliberately distorted to support, for example, anti-Satanic hysteria and those practices that were linked to such fervor.

Consider the verse that read in the original Greek: *thou shalt not suffer a* venefica *to live*. The Latin word *venefica* means *female poisoner*. So the correct translation obviously would be *thou shalt not suffer a* female poisoner *to live*. But King James apparently decided that the term *witch* was synonymous with *poisoner*, so the word *witch* was firmly set into this quote and into the minds of the reading public from that time forward. This incorrect translation became the norm over time and was used to persecute and denigrate multitudes of people. Many paid with their lives.

King James also ensured that the masses would be able to access his Bible in numbers previously unseen. He made the words easy to understand for those with a limited literacy by using a simple Anglo-Saxon vernacular, thus allowing the messages and meanings to be easily read. The King James Bible contains 788,258 words. Of these, only 14,565 are unique. If we compare that to another document from the same period with a similar number of words—the complete works of William Shakespeare, for example (forty-three works between 1589 and 1613)—we find in Shakespeare 884,421 words of which 28,829 are unique word forms. This is nearly twice as many as the King James Bible text. The King James Bible, then, requires a smaller vocabulary making it much simpler to read.

This limited vocabulary became a powerful communications tool, especially when married with the moveable type printing press in Europe at the beginning of the 1600s. The printing press had an ability to produce over 3,600 documents per workday. King James was so anxious to propagate his version of the Bible that he used his own personal printer, Robert Barker, for the task of compiling and distributing the text.

It is clear, then, that some individuals have mistranslated and abused the Bible to force upon the public their own political views and religious doctrines. Because of this, the Bible is not a neutral text devoid of propaganda and bias. This is the deeper context of specific passages often used to attack and admonish the psychic world. For any historian writing a text about the Bible, then, it is sometimes difficult to sift out the untruths and falsehoods that have become established as "fact" over time. Many of these distortions have been set in stone via the King James Bible for over 400 years. Even when proven to be untrue, the distortions persist. Our history is littered with untruths that society now accepts as historically true.

My understanding of art history has made me aware of the way our perceptions have been falsely informed. We perceive that the Virgin Mary, the mother of Christ, wore blue; we see this in every child's nativity play as the young girl playing Mary adorns herself with the clichéd blue blanket. Blue became Mary's color because blue was the most expensive color to create during the Renaissance period. The lapis lazuli required to produce the color blue had to be mined in Afghanistan and shipped back to Italy. Contracts for artwork specifically outlined how much blue would get used in the painting by weight of pigment. So the most important person in Renaissance art, the Madonna, got to wear the most expensive color. This color-coding also reinforced a symbolism that could be understood by the peasantry, who would be able to instantly recognize the Virgin in any painting in any chapel in any town. In much the same way, artistic renderings of St. Peter associated him with the color yellow.

Amazingly, there still remains an incredibly strong argument with insightful evidence to inform us of what the Bible really has to say about the practices of the psychic, medium, healer and paranormal investigator. This book is about you and your path to knowledge. We cannot easily change the prejudices and conventions that Christian society falsely holds, but you can develop an understanding that our practices are perhaps closer to the truth of God's word than what we are handed down.

Blind to the Gospel

In this chapter I show that the Bible I read and love supports and encourages the practices of the psychic and healer throughout the text. Thus I find many to be blind to the teachings of the Gospel and unbelieving of the true content of the Bible because it does not fit with their own personal view. Without actually consulting or analyzing the text, they falsely believe that the Bible could not possibly encourage these activities. We can start by reading the Bible's own statements on this subject.

Matthew 22:29
Jesus replied, "You are in error because you do not know the Scriptures or the power of God."

Jesus expressed this sentiment when he was addressing questions given to him by the Sadducees (a sect of Jews during the Second Temple period) in reference to marital arrangements in the afterlife. It highlights that Jesus was unhappy about the way the Scriptures had been ignored or misinterpreted.

It is easier, of course, to be told what to think rather than to learn how to think; so let us open our eyes and start to see what is actually there. It is the blindness to the actual words of the Bible that I wish to address. In the New Testament, Paul writes letters to Corinth outlining his concern that the teachings of Jesus Christ were being undermined or going unobserved by false ideologies.

2 Corinthians 4:4
The god of this age has blinded the minds of unbelievers, so that they cannot see the light of the gospel that displays the glory of Christ, who is the image of God.

The term *god of this age* in the quote above refers to Satan, not because Satan has any Divine attributes, but because he has the homage of many of the people of this age as their god—as the being who is *really* worshipped, or who has the *true* affection of their hearts. It may be that those who do not believe the gospel are easier subjects for Satan to work on. But it is not just those individuals whose minds are blinded. There are others who cannot see the beauty of the gospel and the true nature of God because of the darkness surrounding them. Experience has shown me that these are the first people to denounce and attack. It was Paul's concern and assiduity towards spreading the true word of the gospel that saw such an increase in Christian followers in the Mediterranean.

I have never experienced the presence of Satan himself during my own work and investigations. But to me he is a very real entity. I have, however, been fortunate enough to witness the presence of an angel. So it would be perfectly reasonable to believe that Satan actually exists, as he is a fallen angel. I have, though, seen non-human entities when on paranormal investigations that I believe to be demonic in nature; the foot soldiers and minions of Satan. These beings also have a hierarchy in the same way angels have a hierarchy. They can be identified by the smell of sulfur, animalistic noises like sniffling and growling, a dark heavy threatening atmosphere that you can almost touch and feel, and in extreme cases the physicality of being attacked in talon-shaped claw marks. The lowest kind of pond life at the bottom of this hierarchy (and the most common I have experienced) has the characteristics of an animal scuttling around the floor at knee height.

Peter, in his writing to the Christian church, criticizes false teachers who distort the authenticity and apostle tradition of the biblical text. Predicting judgment for those individuals, he explains that God has delayed the Second Coming of Christ so that more people have the chance to reject evil and find salvation.

2 Peter 2:10
This is especially true of those who follow the corrupt desire of the flesh and despise authority. Bold and arrogant, they are not afraid to heap abuse on celestial beings.

Those preaching the word of God can also be led to misunderstandings through Satan's hand. They obey Satan's will and execute his plans without even realizing they are being deceived.

Satan has said in numerous places that the kingdoms of the world and their glory are his, and that he gives them to whomsoever he will (Matthew 4:8, Matthew 4:9 and Ephesians 6:12). Remember, Satan has only to tempt some people with dark thoughts. Vice always renders the mind blind and the ego self-important.

Jesus tells us how the word of God is experienced by different people and what their response to it can be when Satan intervenes.

Mark 4:14-15
The farmer sows the word. [15] Some people are like seed along the path, where the word is sown. As soon as they hear it, Satan comes and takes away the word that was sown in them.

So we are told that Satan will come and steal away the word of God if we allow him to do so. This is explained further by Luke.

Luke 8:11-12
This is the meaning of the parable: The seed is the word of God. [12] Those along the path are the ones who hear, and then the devil comes and takes away the word from their hearts, so that they may not believe and be saved.

So why does Satan do this? It is because he is opposed to the Gospel and wishes to prevent its spread and influence in the world. Satan is very much aware that eternal life is only found in the word of God, through our understanding of God's true teaching. Thus Satan and all his arts are being employed to arrest the diffusion of the Gospel on earth through false teachings and created misunderstandings.

The word *light* in the 2 Corinthians 4:4 quote at the beginning of this chapter means excellence, beauty or splendor; light is the emblem of knowledge, purity and innocence and is applied to the Gospel. Light exposes and removes the errors, sins and wretchedness of people just as the light of the sun scatters the darkness of night. Satan will endeavor to accomplish, by all the means in his power, the prevention of the light of the Gospel shining on as many people as possible.

God sends Isaiah to foretell the ruin of his people in the prophecy below and refers to individuals who would understand the truth about God's kingdom. These are the people who would then try to give this information to as many as possible; it's why the word of God is being preached throughout the entire earth. The prophecy also describes the negative attitude of humankind towards this message and the preaching of God's kingdom. The prophet Isaiah, through God, is letting us know the way people would be reacting to the kingdom message. This prophecy is still pertinent to today's society.

Isaiah 6:9-10

He said, "Go and tell this people:

"'Be ever hearing, but never understanding; be ever seeing, but never perceiving.' [12] Make the heart of this people calloused; make their ears dull and close their eyes. Otherwise they might see with their eyes, hear with their ears, understand with their hearts and turn and be healed."

Many hear the sound of God's word, but do not feel the power of it. God sometimes, in righteous judgment, gives men up to blindness of mind, because they will not receive the truth in the love of it. But no humble inquirer after Christ need to fear this awful doom, which is a spiritual judgment on those who will still hold fast their sins.

By a false philosophy which has prevailed due to the blindness many have to the gospel and its true meaning, despite being written for all to see in detail, a part of Christian society seems to have been contrived (as if on purpose) to deceive the world—to destroy the peace and happiness of the people. The dissenters are well conceived and adapted to prostrating the moral power of what they believe is in the Bible: they fetter the intellect, pervert the will, and will make people debased, sunken, polluted and degraded. They see not the light of the sun, the beauty of the landscape or the countenance of a friend; darkness prevails and obscures and they are destitute to beauty. They are empowered to hold the tools that will tarnish your name and your vocation in the name of the Lord; they are put directly before us, and are placed directly between us and the glory of the gospel.

2 Corinthians 11:14-15

"And no wonder, for Satan himself masquerades as an angel of light. It is not surprising, then, if his servants masquerade as servants of righteousness. Their end will be what their actions deserve."

We do not have to be afraid of Satan, though, and his impersonations of the living if we stay away from his dark activities and give our hearts to Jesus.

If you hold doubts that some of what you've learned could be wrong, misinformed, or clouded by the outside influences of darkness, consider the following. In just a very small part of Genesis, I have discovered many worrying inaccuracies in the narrative that I previously believed to be true but were merely common conventions. I was brought up to believe that the animals of the ark went into the boat two-by-two, in other words, as a pair. I even had toys that faithfully recreated the event. I had learned that God delivered the flood in response to his unhappiness towards mankind. It then came as a surprise when I read what the Biblical text actually said about these events.

The Bible clearly states that God was unhappy with the fallen angels (the Nephilim) that came down to earth and impregnated human women to create half-breed fallen angels. This was God's wrath and the focus of the flood. It was then a further insight to find that the majority of the animals (the "clean" animals and the birds) went into the ark in groups of fourteen (seven pairs).

Genesis 6:4
The Nephilim were on the earth in those days—and also afterward—when the sons of God went to the daughters of humans and had children by them.

Genesis 7:2-3
Take with you seven pairs of every kind of clean animal, a male and its mate, and one pair of every kind of unclean animal, a male and its mate, [3] and also seven pairs of every kind of bird, male and female, to keep their various kinds alive throughout the earth.

If something as simple as a few sentences from the Noah's ark story could be so misread and misunderstood by teachers and society in general, what does that suggest about the rest of the text—and other conventions people believe to be true about the more complex issues of ghosts, mediumship and healing?

Also, note that the number seven is an integer with a long history of symbolism associated with it. In the Bible there were *seven* days of creation; anyone who dared to kill Cain would suffer vengeance *seven* times over; there were *seven* years of plenty and *seven* years of famine in the Pharaoh's dream, *seven* days of the feast of Passover, a *seven* day week and pattern of distributing manna; and a *seven* year cycle around the years of Jubilee. Jericho's walls fell on the *seventh* day after *seven* priests with *seven* trumpets marched around the city *seven* times. King David had *seven* older brothers. There were *seven* things that were detestable to the Lord and *seven* pillars of the house of wisdom. These are but a few examples.

The number seven was used within the biblical text because of the importance placed on the integer by older cultures and religions. Buddha walked seven steps at his birth and seven was the number of sages in Hindu mythology, for example. It was also a number that was common in the world during biblical times as seen in the Seven Wonders of the World and the number of celestial objects in the solar system that were visible from earth with the naked eye.

I would now like to consider the idea that Satan would want to deliberately keep the real content and detail of these gospel stories from us. I showed this in my previous examples. It would certainly not be in his interest for us to have a full understanding of what is being taught to us in these passages. So it may not come as a surprise that most people are not aware of the true content of the text. The narrative involving fallen angels (demons) and womankind making love to create a sexual union that would populate the earth with more demonic beings, becomes a lesson in how God destroys the increased population and spread of demonic entities (mankind and his hybrid offspring ultimately destroyed and defeated by God for embracing such liaisons). Obviously Satan wishes to encourage liaisons with mankind to further his ideology and gain more followers.

The ignorance placed upon us by Satan is also reflected in our lack of awareness involving the delineation of clean and unclean animals on the ark. If we are falsely led to believe that all the animals went into the ark two-by-two, then we would have no awareness that there were also clean animals because they went on in seven groups of pairs. So why would Satan not want us to know this detail?

God forbids the consumption of many unclean animals like scavengers and carrion eaters, which devour other animals for their food; pigs, bears, vultures and raptors can eat and thrive on decaying flesh. Predatory animals such as wolves, lions, leopards and cheetahs often prey on the weakest and often diseased members of herds. When it comes to sea creatures, bottom dwellers such as lobsters and crabs scavenge for dead animals on the sea floor. Shellfish such as oysters, clams and mussels similarly consume decaying matter and sewage that sinks to the sea floor.

A common characteristic of many animals God designates as un-clean is that they routinely eat flesh that would sicken or kill human beings. When we eat such animals, we partake of a food chain that includes things harmful to us. It is now possible to see why Satan would want to deceive us into thinking only unclean animals exist-ed, as he also feeds on decay, disease and the weakest. He would also want to promote illness and death throughout the population by man's ignorant consumption of unclean animals. This is why clean animals are removed from the detail of this story in most people's thinking and in popular culture, arguably by the design of dark forces.

It may be suggested that these rules regarding clean and unclean animals no longer apply in contemporary society. But they are still followed and adhered to in the Jewish faith. It also shows you the measure of how affective Satan is at blinding our knowledge of the scriptures. When you consider that this deceit is still ongoing, perhaps ignorance is not our choice in a technologically advanced society.

In re-reading the Noah story, I also realized that I could not re-call the part where Noah was drunk and accidently exposed himself to his children.

Genesis 9:20-22

Noah, a man of the soil, proceeded to plant a vineyard. [21] When he drank some of its wine, he became drunk and lay uncov-ered inside his tent. [22] Ham, the father of Canaan, saw his fa-ther naked and told his two brothers outside.

This story makes Noah human and fallible. It shows that he was not perfect and possessed the human traits of excess and failure—yet God spared him and his family. Noah was chosen because he was the most righteous man on earth (Genesis 7:1 and Ezekiel 14:14). He *walked faithfully with God* (Genesis 6:9), and was a *preacher of righteousness* (2 Peter 2:5). He also showed *godly fear, respect and faith* (Hebrews 11:7).

Satan, I believe, would want you to falsely believe that Noah was perfect to promote the concept that you can only be embraced by God if you are saintly and without sin, thus instilling in people a belief that we will never be close to God because of our own sins and imperfections. This allows Satan to scoop up those in society who feel they are not good enough to be recognized by our Lord or feel they don't qualify.

1 Peter 5:8
Be alert and of sober mind. Your enemy the devil prowls around like a roaring lion looking for someone to devour.

So we must be prepared to let go of what we thought we knew from our previous teachings, knowledge that may have been misinformed or tainted by outside influences.

In conclusion, you can see that the real teaching and word of the Gospel has been hidden from us. Those working as psychics and healers should be aware of this and know that they are acting with the approval of God and against the actions of Satan. You must let go of what you previously believed to be true and open up your mind to a new way of seeing the Word of God.

Talking to Spirits

Deuteronomy 18:9-13 states that the practice of consulting with the dead is detestable to the Lord. This text is often quoted as a reason to express displeasure at the role of the psychic and paranormal investigator. Throughout my career I have experienced a regular level of abuse from all manner of blinded ill-informed individuals, from religious leaders to congregational members and the general public. This has manifested itself in many ways, from posted online videos of admonishing sermons against me, social media hate groups, letters to newspaper editors, and even random verbal attacks in the street. This chapter will teach you that we are actually undertaking God's work and that we should not fear talking to spirits.

As previously discussed when analyzing the King James' version of the Bible, there is a hidden agenda behind much of what is translated in these areas of teaching. Here is the Deuteronomy quote I mentioned in the opening line of this chapter.

Deuteronomy 18:9-13
When you enter the land the LORD your God is giving you, do not learn to imitate the detestable ways of the nations there. [10] Let no one be found among you who sacrifices their son or daughter in the fire, who practices divination or sorcery, interprets omens, engages in witchcraft, [11] or casts spells, or who is a medium or spiritist or who consults the dead. [12] Any-

one who does these things is detestable to the LORD; because of these same detestable practices the LORD your God will drive out those nations before you. [13] You must be blameless before the LORD your God.

These words are not damning the psychic as they first appear. I will break this text down sentence by sentence to give you the true meaning, which must be understood in the context of the time. It states that those who follow pagan ways (the Egyptians and the Romans with their multi-deities, for example) will not be welcomed by God into the Promised Land: "thou shalt have no other Gods." Sorcery (the use of power gained from the assistance or control of spirits, especially for divining) can play a significant part in pagan traditions, so it is also condemned. In some pagan practices spells are also used to change future paths or to make individuals pursue tasks not of their free will. These practices are not in keeping with an ideology in which we are at God's mercy or under His will or command. So this aspect of the text would not appear to be unreasonable if you exercise your skills outside of God's Word. Remember that every practice undertaken must be achieved through consultation with God.

Isaiah 8:20
Consult God's instruction and the testimony of warning. If anyone does not speak according to this word, they have no light of dawn.

Genesis 35:2
So Jacob said to his household and to all who were with him, "Get rid of the foreign gods you have with you, and purify yourselves and change your clothes."

We will now look more closely at the context of Deuteronomy. This book consists of three sermons delivered to the Israelites by Moses on the plains of Moab, shortly before they entered the Promised Land. The first sermon recaps the forty years of wilderness wanderings which have led to this moment and ends with an exhortation to observe the law (or teachings) of God. The second sermon reminds the Israelites of the need for an *exclusive allegiance* to God and observance of the laws He has given them, the conditions on which their possession of the land depends. The third sermon declares that all will be restored upon the act of repentance should Israel lose the land due to unfaithfulness.

Based on this context, let us deal with the medium and spiritualist aspects first. God's concern in the text was with those who practice the worship of other gods and deities. So He is referring to the work of mediums and spiritualists who use other gods and spirits to find their information. The passage below clearly indicates this. Molek (or Moloch) is the name of an ancient Ammonite god that was worshipped by the Canaanites, Phoenicians and related cultures in North Africa. Moloch had associations with a particular kind of propitiatory child sacrifice undertaken by the parents. An association by psychics and spiritists with this god would naturally be seen as unacceptable, and as such denounced.

Leviticus 20:1-6

The Lord said to Moses, [2] "Say to the Israelites: 'Any Israelite or any foreigner residing in Israel who sacrifices any of his children to Molek is to be put to death. The members of the community are to stone him. [3] I myself will set my face against him and will cut him off from his people; for by sacrificing his children to Molek, he has defiled my sanctuary and profaned my holy name. [4] If the members of the community close their eyes when that man sacrifices one of his children to Molek and if they fail to put him to death, [5] I myself will set my face against him and his family and will cut them off from their people together with all who follow him in prostituting themselves to Molek.

[6] "'I will set my face against anyone who turns to mediums and spiritists to prostitute themselves by following them, and I will cut them off from their people.

The following text indicates within the framework of Deuteronomy that the sole opposition to the work of the psychic (the term prophet is used within the passage), is the promotion of other gods through those skills. The actual process of being a psychic is never criticized or attacked.

Deuteronomy 13:1-3

If a prophet, or one who foretells by dreams, appears among you and announces to you a sign or wonder, ² and if the sign or wonder spoken of takes place, and the prophet says, "Let us follow other gods" (gods you have not known) "and let us worship them," ³ you must not listen to the words of that prophet or dreamer.

The passage is denouncing mediums and spiritualists because of *who* they were actually asking for that assistance rather than denouncing the *process* of asking. We can then understand in that context why God proceeds to outline the following. These statements reflect the danger of practicing being a psychic through pagan gods. If we work through God they do not refer to us.

Leviticus 20:27

A man or woman who is a medium or spiritist among you must be put to death. You are to stone them; their blood will be on their own heads.

Leviticus 19:26

Do not practice divination or seek omens.

Leviticus 19:31

Do not turn to mediums or seek out spiritists, for you will be defiled by them. I am the LORD YOUR GOD.

In a further reinforcement of this command we can see another example of how God does not want you to practice psychic skills through other gods. God fervently attacks King Manasseh for his pagan ways. Manasseh had practiced the art of divination and prophecy in connection with child sacrifice and the worship of pagan gods.

2 Kings 21:6
He sacrificed his own son in the fire, practiced divination, sought omens, and consulted mediums and spiritists. He did much evil in the eyes of the LORD, AROUSING HIS ANGER.

I have clearly shown that God is not attacking or denouncing the process of divination or talking to spirits. He is solely concerned with how you are coming by that information and which gods you are working through to make that happen. Let us now deal with the part of Deuteronomy that reads: *consults the dead*. We must first acknowledge that the Bible clearly tells us that spirits do actually exist.

1 Corinthians 15:50
I declare to you, brothers and sisters, that flesh and blood cannot inherit the kingdom of God, nor does the perishable inherit the imperishable.

This is an interesting quote, because it states that only the *spirit* will enter into heaven. It is true from personal experience that I do not normally see decayed human flesh during my readings. Decay is of the body, and the body has long since separated from the spirit. I have found, though, that spirits tend to present themselves to me in the form they had occupied when they were happiest in their lifetime. Grandma can appear as a hot young woman from the 1950s instead of an octogenarian with no teeth and a false hip.

Clearly there is a spirit within each of us. Our first step, then, is to understand that spirits actually exist around us and that we can communicate with them. Remember that *God is Spirit*, and you and I are spirit, too. Communicating with God, therefore, takes place on a spiritual level. We are so inundated and stimulated with the constant noise of the physical, however, that it is difficult to be aware that the spirit exists. To have clarity, it seems best to silence the noise from the physical plane. That is what *being still* is all about.

Psalm 46:10
He says, "Be still, and know that I am God."

When you still the body, quiet the mind, and focus on the spiritual connection you have with God, thoughts will come to you. Some of those thoughts may be from God and some may not. Your expectations of God will play a large part in how you determine which thoughts are actually from God. In a state of meditation, outside thoughts can be removed or reduced. We are then in a better position to receive thoughts that are imprinted into our minds from outside sources. We can identify these from our own thoughts by the random nature of these images—a thought that is without any previous context, for example, or a message that is unconnected or unrelated to anything we have experienced leading up to that meditation. If we are meditating on God, having brought God's love into our life, and if we have protected and spiritually cleansed our environment, then we should have faith that the message is from God.

When we pray to God to enable us to access spirits, it allows us to differentiate from where those messages are coming. If we have doubts about the clarity of our message we can simply wipe the whiteboard that is our mind clear, and ask for a confirmation. This can be done many times. If during a psychic reading I receive important life-changing information for a client from a deceased loved one, then I want to make sure I get the message right. I will spend several minutes meditating on that message and I will keep asking the spirit to clarify and to reinforce what I am to relay.

Studying the Bible and reflecting on the ideas you have about God will impact how you define what is *from God*. God alone knows our thoughts, our hearts, our words and our actions.

1 Corinthians 2:7-8
No, we declare God's wisdom, a mystery that has been hidden and that God destined for our glory before time began. [8] None of the rulers of this age understood it, for if they had, they would not have crucified the Lord of glory.

Psalms 94:11
The Lord knows all human plans...

Psalms 139:3-4
You discern my going out and my laying down; you are familiar with all my ways. [4] Before a word is on my tongue you, LORD, know it completely.

These passages highlight that God knows every hair on our head and is fully aware of our thoughts and actions. It is stated further in Matthew and John that Jesus also knew the thoughts of man.

Matthew 12:25
Jesus knew their thoughts and said to them, "Every kingdom divided against itself will be ruined, and every city or household divided against itself will not stand".

John 10:27
(Jesus) My sheep listen to my voice; I know them, and they follow me.

Other beings can also deliver messages to us through thoughts and in spirit, including angels.

Hebrews 1:14
Are not all angels ministering spirits sent to serve those who will inherit salvation?

Psalms 103:20
Praise the Lord, you his angels, you mighty ones who do his bidding, who obey his word.

Matthew 2:13
When they had gone, an angel of the Lord appeared to Joseph in a dream. "Get up," he said, "take the child and his mother

and escape to Egypt. Stay there until I tell you, for Herod is going to search for the child to kill him."

These messages can be relayed to us outside of meditations. They can be experienced in dreams, impressions, visualizations, or during any random circumstance, as highlighted previously with my own Divine encounters. We can communicate with God, angels, and spirits with our thoughts. This is called being clairvoyant—able to see beyond the range of ordinary perception. The word derives from the French *clair,* meaning clear and *voyant,* to see; *clear seeing.* Practicing meditation techniques and keeping a dream journal will help you to access and remember these messages. Please be aware that Satan can also speak to us through our thoughts and we must protect ourselves against such pollution. Remember he is an angel too. But Satan does not know what we are thinking—as we have been told, only God knows this.

The ability to hear spirits without seeing them is also revealed as a Biblical practice. This is called clairaudience.

Acts 9:7
The men traveling with Saul stood there speechless; they heard the sound but did not see anyone.

Spirits, the Bible tells us, exist and communicate with us through psychic means. So now let us address the passages from Deuteronomy and other parts of the Bible that tell us we should not talk to the dead.

The Bible has told us that we move in spirit to heaven and will continue to have an existence there. Consulting with other spirits in that realm would not be construed as consulting with the dead. The following text tells us that we do not actually die, but rather move to a new place, and there will be no more death.

Revelation 21:3-4
And I heard a loud voice from the throne saying, "Look! God's dwelling place is now among the people, and he will dwell

with them. They will be his people, and God himself will be with them and be their God. ⁴ 'He will wipe every tear from their eyes. There will be no more death' or mourning or crying or pain, for the old order of things has passed away."

To put the death, spirit and ghost controversy into perspective, it's important to understand the Bible's teaching on life after death. The scripture explains that when we leave this physical realm we are judged and our spirits will go to either heaven or hell.

Hebrews 9:27
Just as people are destined to die once, and after that to face judgment...

There are several scriptures that highlight this and tell us that we are immediately in the presence of the Lord.

2 Corinthians 5:8
We are confident, I say, and would prefer to be away from the body and at home with the Lord.

In the following passage from Philippians, Paul discusses his desire to "depart" and to be with Christ. Interestingly, he does not use the term to "die."

Philippians 1:23
I am torn between the two: I desire to depart and be with Christ, which is better by far;

Jesus also spoke to the thief on the cross and told him that one day He would be with him in Paradise.

The Bible tells us that a spiritual realm, invisible to human eyes, does exist, so who, then, actually dies? Well, according to the Bible, death is reserved for those who sin or do wrong in the eyes of the Lord. They will not be welcomed into His spiritual land. Remember, hell is a place where God is *not*! The passages below outline the concept that only the sinner will die.

Ezekiel 18:4

For everyone belongs to me, the parent as well as the child—both alike belong to me. The one who sins is the one who will die.

Romans 5:12

Therefore, just as sin entered the world through one man, and death through sin, and in this way death came to all people, because all sinned.

Genesis 2:17

"...but you must not eat from the tree of the knowledge of good and evil, for when you eat from it you will certainly die."

The second death, as described in Revelation, is an eternal punishment in the lake of fire, experienced only by the unsaved, who die once in the physical realm and then for a second time in hell. An eternal separation is now made between those who have life in spirit and those who have death in spirit.

Revelation 20:14

Then death and Hades were thrown into the lake of fire. The lake of fire is the second death.

We have now established that the only way we die in spirit is to be sent to hell, and those that are believers will have eternal life. I now want to suggest, based on Biblical fact, that eternal life in spirit can have more than one physical life in this realm, implying the concept of past lives but with one and the same spirit. I have seen during my readings that previous lives play an important role in people's current lives. I have been given information by the deceased that has shown me what the spirit of a client has done in a previous life. I have looked deeply into my own spirit and received information on my own previous incarnations, and have experienced the way it influences my life.

These past life experiences can be shown in the skills that we have brought with us into this life without good cause or reason. In my own life I have discovered from the first moment I was given a pencil, as a small child, that I could draw better than any of my peers, with a knowledge of perspective and other formalistic skills beyond my years and without guidance or instruction. I also found that when I picked up a sword it felt like an extension of my arm and I was able to use it in a skilled and accomplished way. I subsequently fenced to a high level and represented my county at the sport as captain of my team. The first time I ever sat on a horse I was somehow aware of what I needed to do and it felt familiar and natural. These are just a few examples from introspectively examining my own life that I can give for having a natural affinity or skill that could have been brought from previous lives, as you will be able to do with your own life experiences.

We can also look at what we have brought with us that scares us, or causes us concern, our phobias and fears. I have a dislike for having sticky hands, not to the point of having to wash them all the time in a compulsive manner, but just a real nauseating nagging in my mind such as when I have an ice-cream cone on a hot day and my hands are tacky. It will pick and pull at my conscious thinking until I find an opportunity to wash them. I always thought this to be an odd sensation that seemed to be without justification. But I have already established that I believe I have fought as a warrior with a sword, and was a skilled horseman. It would then be reasonable to assume that at some point in the distant past I was engaged in hand-to-hand combat in battle, with the blood of heavy fighting running down my sword and subsequently over my hands, making them sticky. I believe then that my unhappiness at having sticky hands derives from the residual memories I have triggered of my time in bloody conflict.

I also have a phobia of spiders that even in my educated introspective reasoning cannot be easily explained as I have never had a bad experience with one. Yet I stay away from them and they cause me to have a physical fear reaction. I suspect I may have been killed by a spider bite in another period of history, in another part of the world. It is possible that people's phobias of heights, water and snakes, for example, could derive from past life experiences, before their current incarnations. This concept would also account for the feelings we have of Déjà vu and the phenomena of meeting someone for the first time but having the sensation that you know them intimately and have met before.

To reinforce these ideas, I have spoken to spirits and they have made me aware that they have the ability to come and go as they please. You have choices that you can make once you are in spirit. You can choose to create a realistic world for yourself in any time frame with any property, location or individuals in spirit. You can then choose to dip into this physical realm to see relatives and friends that are still present in that realm. Or you can choose to come back and have another go at life, with the same spirit in a different physical body, perhaps with a different gender, race or nationality. This idea would initially seem to go against what we believe to be the teaching of God's word in the Bible. But this would be incorrect, as the Bible clearly states that we can have many lives.

This concept is highlighted when the disciples ask Jesus in the book of John who committed the sin for a blind man to be born blind; the man or his parents?

John 9:1-2
As he went along, he saw a man blind from birth. 2 His disciples asked him, "Rabbi, who sinned, this man or his parents, that he was born blind?"

As the child was born blind, it would suggest that they meant the sin occurred in a previous life. Jesus then has an opportunity to denounce the possibility of reincarnation here, but does not do so.

On another occasion Nicodemus asks Jesus about the idea of being born again and reincarnation. Nicodemus does not understand what Jesus is telling him and he is confused by the concept of getting back into the womb for a second time. Jesus explains to Nicodemus that it will be the spirt that will again unite into flesh the next time.

John 3:1-8

Now there was a Pharisee, a man named Nicodemus who was a member of the Jewish ruling council. [2] He came to Jesus at night and said, "Rabbi, we know that you are a teacher who has come from God. For no one could perform the signs you are doing if God were not with him."

[3] Jesus replied, "Very truly I tell you, no one can see the kingdom of God unless they are born again."

[4] "How can someone be born when they are old?" Nicodemus asked. "Surely they cannot enter a second time into their mother's womb to be born!"

[5] Jesus answered, "Very truly I tell you, no one can enter the kingdom of God unless they are born of water and the Spirit. [6] Flesh gives birth to flesh, but the Spirit gives birth to spirit. [7] You should not be surprised at my saying, 'You must be born again.' [8] The wind blows wherever it pleases. You hear its sound, but you cannot tell where it comes from or where it is going. So it is with everyone born of the Spirit."

A further example can be shown when Jesus visits the villages around Caesarea Philippi and asks his disciples who the villagers think he is. They answered that the people thought he was either John the Baptist (who had been beheaded by then), Elijah (who was dead) or one of the deceased prophets.

Mark 8:27-28

Jesus and his disciples went on to the villages around Caesarea Philippi. On the way he asked them, "Who do people say I am?"

[28] They replied, "Some say John the Baptist; others say Elijah; and still others, one of the prophets."

Apparently the population believed in reincarnation, and once more one might expect Jesus to tell the disciples that the people were wrong in that belief. But He does not do so. Instead, the next verse tells us that Jesus then asks His disciples, "But whom say ye that I am?" And this is answered by Peter in his *Confession of Christ*, in which Peter says: "Thou art the Christ."

In the passage below Jesus describes John the Baptist as the prophet Elijah reborn. This is another reference to reincarnation from the lips of Jesus himself.

Matthew 11:11-15

Truly I tell you, among those born of women there has not risen anyone greater than John the Baptist; yet whoever is least in the kingdom of heaven is greater than he. [12] From the days of John the Baptist until now, the kingdom of heaven has been subjected to violence, and violent people have been raiding it. [13] For all the Prophets and the Law prophesied until John. [14] And if you are willing to accept it, he is the Elijah who was to come. [15] Whoever has ears, let them hear.

We have already discussed how the influential King James Bible purposely mistranslated specific words to keep with an agenda. This is also the case with the theme of reincarnation. The following passage comes from Isaiah.

Isaiah 53:9

He was assigned a grave with the wicked, and with the rich in his death, though he had done no violence, nor was any deceit in his mouth.

The word *death* used in this verse was originally *deaths* when translated from Hebrew. "And he made his grave with the wicked, and with the rich in his deaths." This raises the question of why the translators in 1611 decided to change the word. This original meaning would clearly indicate that reincarnation exists, as the word death could not be considered to be a plural number if reincarnation did not exist.

It could be suggested, then, that Jesus believed in reincarnation. His teachers also believed in it, the early church believed in it, and the local population believed in it. So why would those controlling the translation of the Bible seek to remove the elements that suggest reincarnation exists? This is answered when you consider the idea that if you control people's beliefs, then you will control the people. If it is proven that it is God alone that has power over them and they could die and come back, then that also undermines the monarchy and rulers. And as we know, King James was a monarch that personally oversaw the translation process and agenda.

Elements that refer to reincarnation were also removed from the canon of the Bible that we know today. These documents were taken away in the fourth century and then lost to the knowledge of man. One of these texts was then unearthed in 1945 at the base of a cliff in Nag Hammadi in Egypt. It is believed that its contents and teachings were removed from the Bible due to their gnostic nature by literalists who were condemning and removing what they thought were heretical writings.

This discarded text suggests that reincarnation was part of early Biblical teaching. An example of that can be seen in the Apocryphon of John (translated as the secret teaching of John), found twice in the Nag Hammadi library. In this text, the author (taking the persona of John) describes a vision after the teacher has ascended. The heavens appear to open and a being descends, whom the text says is "the Spirit" and to whom John puts questions, often addressing him as "Christ." This Divine teacher at one point expresses a teaching which appears to establish a doctrine of reincarnation.

> I said, "Christ, when the souls leave the flesh, where will they go?" He laughed and said to me, "To a place of the soul, which is the power that is greater than the counterfeit spirit. This (soul) is powerful. It flees from the works of wickedness and it is saved by the incorruptible oversight and brought up to the repose of the aeons." I said, "Christ, what about those who do not know the All -- what are their souls or where will they go?" He said to me, "In those, a counterfeit spirit proliferated by causing them to stumble. And in that way he burdens their

soul and draws it into works of wickedness, and he leads it into forgetfulness. After it has become naked in this way, he hands it over to the authorities who came into being from the Ruler. And again they cast them into fetters. And they consort with them until they are saved from forgetfulness and it receives some knowledge. And in this way, it becomes perfect and is saved." I said, "Christ, how does the soul become smaller and enter again into the nature of the mother or the human?" He rejoiced when I asked this, and he said, "Blessed are you for paying close attention!"

This passage can certainly be interpreted as teaching the possibility of multiple incarnations. It is interesting to further note that it says that the souls of those who do not yet "know the All" after they leave the flesh, undergo "forgetfulness." This would account for our current spirit not knowing any other physical form outside of the one it currently resides in. Christ then explains the way the soul is cast again into an incarnation: "another who has the Spirit of Life in it," and can follow and obey and then "be saved," after which "of course it does not enter into another flesh."

So we have a choice to reincarnate and come back to the physical realm, or we can spend an eternal life in spirit. Eternal life is mentioned so often in the Bible (45 times), and is such a constant narrative, that anyone familiar with the Bible must have surely questioned what the term "being dead" actually means.

John 11:25-26
Jesus said to her, "I am the resurrection and the life. The one who believes in me will live, even though they die; [26] and whoever lives by believing in me will never die. Do you believe this?"

Revelations 21:3-4
And I heard a loud voice from the throne saying, "Look! God's dwelling place is now among the people, and he will dwell

with them. They will be his people, and God himself will be
with them and be their God. ⁴'He will wipe every tear from
their eyes. There will be no more death' or mourning or crying or pain, for the old order of things has passed away.''

Ezekiel 18:31
Rid yourselves of all the offenses you have committed, and get
a new heart and a new spirit. Why will you die, people of Israel?

Romans 6:23
For the wages of sin is death, but the gift of God is eternal life
in Christ Jesus our Lord.

So if we are told not to talk to the dead, is the Bible using the
term "dead" as a reference to anyone who ends up in hell, as this
is now the only place where we can actually die? So any psychic
communication attempted with spirits languishing in hell would not
only be prohibited because these are the dead we are told not to
engage with, but would also prove to be impossible as the spirits
are now deceased. The word "dead" in this context cannot be solely
dismissed as purely semantics based on the evidence presented and
the frequency of the term *eternal life*. We can see in the verses below
that only those vanquished to hell will die.

Matthew 10:28
Do not be afraid of those who kill the body but cannot kill the
soul. Rather, be afraid of the One who can destroy both soul
and body in hell.

Acts 2:25-27
David said about Him:

I saw the Lord always before me. Because he is at my right
hand, I will not be shaken. ²⁶Therefore my heart is glad and

my tongue rejoices; my body also will rest in hope, [27] because you will not abandon me to the realm of the dead, you will not let your holy one see decay.

We now have Biblical confirmation that spirits exist in heaven. We are told that the reward for a sin-free life is entry into God's land for eternity. It is my belief that in heaven, through the will of God, we interact with those who have eternal life in spirit. The John 3:16 text is often held up and displayed at sporting events and is very well known. But we can easily miss the depth of what this verse is actually saying—that we are not going to die if we embrace God's love.

John 3:16
For God so loved the world that he gave his one and only Son, that whoever believes in him shall not perish but have eternal life.

This concept is further reinforced later in the text, but we are now told that death awaits those in spirit who reject the Gospel.

John 3:36
Whoever believes in the Son has eternal life, but whoever rejects the Son will not see life, for God's wrath remains on them.

The following passage reinforces the belief that there is a spirit inside every one of us, and that the spirit is aware of the person's thoughts and feelings. Thus if one can contact the spirit that resided within the person (when the physical flesh and bones have long since gone), the deceased persons' thoughts, life and memories can be revealed. The following text is my favorite section of the Bible and Paul is the author I enjoy reading the most. In his youth he attended the school of Gamaliel in Jerusalem where he received an extensive education in classical literature, philosophy and ethics. This elevates his writing skills beyond the other authors of the New Testament who were first and foremost a fisherman, tax collector and physician. In many ways this entire book has been written around the following verses.

1 Corinthians 12:1-11
Now about the gifts of the Spirit, brothers and sisters, I do not want you to be uninformed. [2]You know that when you were pagans, somehow or other you were influenced and led astray to mute idols. [3]Therefore I want you to know that no one who is speaking by the Spirit of God says, "Jesus be cursed," and no one can say, "Jesus is Lord," except by the Holy Spirit.

[4]There are different kinds of gifts, but the same Spirit distributes them. [5]There are different kinds of service, but the same Lord. [6]There are different kinds of working, but in all of them and in everyone it is the same God at work.

[7]Now to each one the manifestation of the Spirit is given for the common good. [8]To one there is given through the Spirit a message of wisdom, to another a message of knowledge by means of the same Spirit, [9]to another faith by the same Spirit, to another gifts of healing by that one Spirit, [10]to another miraculous powers, to another prophecy, to another distinguishing between spirits, to another speaking in different kinds of tongues, and to still another the interpretation of tongues.[11]All these are the work of one and the same Spirit, and he distributes them to each one, just as he determines.

Paul warns us not to be ignorant to the facts he is about to reveal: *I do not want you to be uninformed.* He tells us that if we use the gifts he mentions, we are obeying his Word and Gospel: *there are different kinds of working, but in all of them and in everyone it is the same God at work.* Paul then proceeds to tell us that it is a gift to us from God to go and help our fellow man: *now to each one the manifestation of the Spirit is given for the common good.* He tells us that those gifts should not be questioned, so any opposition toward the psychic or healer should be removed at this point.

The gifts mentioned include obtaining wisdom and knowledge gained via messages from the spirit; one person may be given a message of wisdom, and a second person given a message of knowledge by means of the same Spirit. The gift of healing may also be given to some by that one Spirit. We are told that miraculous powers and prophecy are also bestowed upon some by the Lord, but to others miraculous powers, and to still others the gift of prophecy, or the ability to differentiate and know spirits, or to distinguish between spirits.

These gifts are distributed to individuals as God sees fit. At his discretion, *all these are the work of one and the same Spirit, and he distributes them to each one, just as he determines.* The passage tells us that each man has received individual gifts and is required to go out and develop those gifts into skills. Remember that God has plans for all of us to help our fellow man and to deliver us from evil.

Jeremiah 29:11
"For I know the plans I have for you," declares the Lord, "plans to prosper you and not to harm you, plans to give you hope and a future."

So we are left to believe that anyone who does not embrace those skills is not delivering on God's word. This could ultimately result in a day of reckoning where one stands before God who asks, "Why did you never use your gifts to help your fellow man?"

The words in Corinthians may be the most important words written in the Bible to provide evidence that God wishes us to use the gifts he has given us, including the gifts of healing, mediumship, and the receiving of messages from the spirits. We must remind ourselves that our gifts are from God and should not be given up or left idle. They are ultimately your birthright, so do not throw away what is yours through misadventure or sin; use what you have been given. Do not give it up or keep it repressed and hidden. The following story of Esau and Jacob reflects this sentiment perfectly.

Genesis 25:27-34

The boys grew up, and Esau became a skillful hunter, a man of the open country, while Jacob was content to stay at home among the tents. [28] Isaac, who had a taste for wild game, loved Esau, but Rebekah loved Jacob.

[29] Once when Jacob was cooking some stew, Esau came in from the open country, famished. [30] He said to Jacob, "Quick, let me have some of that red stew! I'm famished!" (That is why he was also called Edom.])

[31] Jacob replied, "First sell me your birthright."

[32] "Look, I am about to die," Esau said. "What good is the birthright to me?"

[33] But Jacob said, "Swear to me first." So he swore an oath to him, selling his birthright to Jacob.

[34] Then Jacob gave Esau some bread and some lentil stew. He ate and drank, and then got up and left.

You also have been given a birthright by having gifts placed upon you by God. Stay true to what you have been given. We are blessed with God-given gifts which are our birthright. To not use those gifts to help your fellow man would go against the wishes of our Lord. Esau despised his birthright. He was unaware of the enormity of what he was blessed with and was willing to give it up. He did not care. He gave up everything for a bowl of stew.

Luke 9:24-25

For whoever wants to save their life will lose it, but whoever loses their life for me will save it. [25] What good is it for someone to gain the whole world, and yet lose or forfeit their very self?

We have discussed that God admonishes those who follow pagan deities and practices in the name of false gods and that spirits exist and we can interact with them because God has given us the gift to do so. We have learned that those who "die" are the spirits that sinned when they had access to a physical form here on earth, and we cannot interact with them. So let's look at what spirits can offer us in terms of knowledge.

The following Bible story recognizes that fortune telling is possible. This story is about Paul and Silas who end up in prison for removing a slave girl's fortune telling skills much to the consternation of her owner.

Act 16:16

Once when we were going to the place of prayer, we were met by a female slave who had a spirit by which she predicted the future. An acknowledgment of a spirit She earned a great deal of money for her owners by fortune-telling. Then is money not the issue

[17] She followed Paul and the rest of us, shouting, "These men are servants of the Most High God, who are telling you the way to be saved."

[18] She kept this up for many days. Finally Paul became so annoyed that he turned around and said to the spirit, "In the name of Jesus Christ I command you to come out of her!" At that moment the spirit left her.

I like this story; it is another acknowledgment that if you have a spirit with you (or, indeed, the Holy Spirit) then mediumship is possible. Remember that Paul reacted this way because she was annoying, not because of her gifts. It acknowledges the gift of psychic thoughts through the engagement of a spirit; in this way, communicating with a spirit to gain knowledge and foresight is acknowledged by the Bible as fact. Paul does not punish the female slave for using her gift, so it would appear not to be important to the teachings of God, otherwise this would have been the perfect opportunity to chastise the slave girl for doing so. The slave actually wants to promote God's word and help raise the profile of Paul in his mission. It is then evident that you can interact with a spirit and still be with God. It is only because the slave annoys Paul that he acts; there is no rebuttal or denigration of the girl due to her calling.

This passage also shows that patience was a virtue Paul even struggled to master, as the slave did indeed test the patience of a saint. A careful reading of the passage shows that the spirits are subject to the will of the word of Christ; so through Christ, communications with spirits is accepted and possible.

There are other parts of the Bible that tell us more about the role of the dead and emphasize that we are not meant to be engaging with those that are "dead in spirit." Here is an example of that teaching.

Isaiah 8:19
When someone tells you to consult mediums and spiritists, who whisper and mutter, should not a people inquire of their God? Why consult the dead on behalf of the living?

This verse poses this question: why consult those that are in hell on behalf of those that are in heaven or are still on earth? "Consultation," of course, suggests a dialogue involving answers to questions. In my experience, when undertaking communications with the spirits, the client is usually searching for reassurances and one last precious moment with his or her deceased loved one; the client normally receives a reinforcement of love and tenderness and some shared childhood memories or recollections. In my experience, spirits cannot tell me anything of the future. The spirits only know information that they knew in life, and from what they have seen and experienced when visiting this realm from their spirit world. They can tell you where the buried the money is but not which horse to bet it on. They know what we know—certainly not the lottery numbers.

The Bible actually provides us with a list from God that describes those He sees worthy of attaining a place in heaven.

1 Corinthians 12:28
And God has placed in the church first of all apostles, second prophets, third teachers, then miracles, then gifts of healing, of helping, of guidance, and of different kinds of tongues.

As psychics working through God, as teachers passing on knowledge, and as healers who wish to help and give guidance through our work, we should be encouraged that we are included in this list at second, third, fifth, sixth and seventh places—behind such elevated company as apostles. It appears that God obviously respects and rewards what we do.

I now want to give you an insight into the experiences I have gained from accessing the spirit world. When I work with a client to specifically find a departed relative or friend, I first ask for the deceased's name. This allows me to go and speak straight to the spirit rather than just opening myself up to anyone who wants to come along. If I opened myself up in a non-specific way to access spirits I would expect random individuals to come through, perhaps linked to the history of the property I am working in, or spirits known remotely to my client, like a distant neighbor or work colleague from years ago. Although I have experience of this phenomena, my clients normally come to me wanting to connect with a very specific individual in spirit.

If my client has booked the reading several weeks in advance it is common for the spirit they wish to contact to come and visit me before the reading. The spirit is normally aware that we are going to talk and is overly enthusiastic, wanting to give me as much information as possible before the appointment. I could be in the car or even in the shower when that individual in spirit comes and introduces themselves to me. It is not uncommon to start a session by providing a page of information and messages from the spirit when the client arrives.

I have discovered that when I am asked to access deceased loved ones, I normally find them participating in the acts they would have enjoyed when they were alive—gardening, baking, playing golf, fishing, messing around in a garage with an old car, etc. I ask the client who they wish to contact. I will then go looking for them by opening myself up and asking God to find them for me. I then get to see clairvoyantly where they are, almost as if I am led by the hand in my third eye to the property or location they are residing at in spirit. I may find myself standing outside of a workshop, or at the threshold of a kitchen, or in the middle of a manicured lawn looking at a well-tended garden. I then explain to the living relative—a daughter, for example—what activity the spirit is engaged with. Then I say to the spirit, "I have your daughter with me and she would like to talk with you." The client will tell me how much that person enjoyed that activity when they were in the physical realm. So my initial interaction with my client is normally based on a description of what the spirit looks like and where I have found them. The client can normally recognize the environment from a period in their own history or childhood.

In my experience I find spirits are able to create a spirit world around them in a reality of their choosing. So if the spirit was happiest in a house they lived in during the 1960s, then that is where I will find them. Imagine your perfect environment of when you were the happiest in your life and the age at which you were the happiest. I am regularly asked to contact the deceased grandmothers of my clients. As previously mentioned, they tend to come through to me as beautiful twenty-one-year-olds in period 1950s figure-hugging dresses with bright-red ruby lipstick—not how the family recalls them in their old age. I remember one reading where the client's father even came to me as an eight year old boy, a time when he was the happiest and how he wanted to present himself. All pain is also removed when we are in spirit, and cancers or illnesses are gone. Individuals have even appeared with a full complement of limbs, when in the physical realm they had lost an arm or a leg.

Not only can you create your own perfect environment around you, and how you wish to be seen, but you can also reunite with your deceased friends and relatives. It has been my experience that during an interaction with a spirit for a client, other deceased family members and friends will make themselves known to me. On occasion it is the deceased person that has gone to get them in the spirit world so they can acknowledge the presence of others to the client. This is also true of pets. I have seen dogs, cats, rabbits, and even a horse with the owner who has passed on. It is normally a good sign when a dog in spirit comes bounding into the room because it indicates that the owner will not be far behind. This is similar to the physical realm in which a dog will run to the front door or gate to greet you before the owner arrives.

The only time I find I cannot access a spirit is when they do not wish to talk with the client, so they have obstinately refused to engage with me, despite the fact that I can see them and can describe them to the client. Some spirits still carry their feuds and feelings into the spirit world and harbor old wounds and disagreements with those who are still living. Thus they refuse to talk with family members or friends that are living. During these moments (and it has only happened on a few occasions) I will tell the client that the spirit does not wish to talk to them. This they fully understand based on the relationship they had with that spirit when they were in the physical realm.

I would not for one moment just sit there and make it up, and I have no problem with saying let's try again in a few months. During that intervening time I may ask my client to talk out loud to the spirit they wish to communicate with to clear the air, perhaps by saying what needs to be said in the car when they are on their own, or by verbalizing their thoughts at home so the spirit can hear them. This has proven to be successful on several occasions, as the spirit has then been willing to talk when a second session was subsequently organized.

We have the same personality traits, drives, and desires in the spirit world as we do in this physical realm. I once heard a spirit trying to communicate with a blue-eyed blond-haired member of my paranormal investigation team via a piece of equipment called a ghost box. This device scans radio frequencies very quickly in a loop and generates white noise which is believed to aid communication with the spirit world. The building was the site of a Wild West type saloon bar and hotel, and the spirit that came through was very much of that era. He blatantly came out and asked the lady in question to *take her top off*. She firmly replied *no*, to which the spirit responded by saying *please*.

I have also experienced the phenomena of having a series of prolonged conversations with the deceased female owner of a building I was investigating. We got on so well during these dialogues that one could say that we were quite blatantly flirting with each other. It got to the point where other investigation teams, that were independently investigating the building, would tell me that she came through and asked where I was. I will continue to chat this lady up until someone tells me that it is illegal to flirt with somebody who died in 1933.

To summarize, this chapter has shown us that the Bible actually promotes the idea of talking to spirits to gain wisdom and knowledge from them. We are told that we have been given the gifts of healing and prophecy, and these gifts have to be used for the welfare of our fellow man. We are told our skills are not meant to be questioned and that God will reward us with a specific place in heaven for using them. We have proven through Biblical verses that past lives and reincarnation are possible and that we have eternal life in God's embrace. When we are told not to engage with the dead, the Bible is actually referring to those in hell who have solely died in spirit. This is very conclusive and poses the question as to why so many Christians are opposed to the work we engage in.

Ghosts and Hauntings

I have been told by the more conservative practitioners of the Christian faith that the Bible informs us ghosts do not exist, and neither do hauntings (or that they are the work of Satan). However, this concept is not grounded in Biblical fact. In the King James Bible the term *ghost* is actually used 108 times. So let me start by saying that ghosts do exist. They are a visual incarnation of a spirit and we have already learned that spirits exist. So the existence of ghosts should not really come as a surprise. Here are a few places where ghosts are mentioned.

1 Samuel 28:13
The king said to her, "Don't be afraid. What do you see?" The woman said, "I see a **ghost**ly figure coming up out of the earth."

Isaiah 29:4
Brought low, you will speak from the ground; your speech will mumble out of the dust. Your voice will come **ghost**like from the earth; out of the dust your speech will whisper.

Matthew 14:26
When the disciples saw him walking on the lake, they were terrified. "It's a **ghost**," they said, and cried out in fear.

Mark 6:49

...but when they saw him walking on the lake, they thought he was a **ghost**. They cried out...

Luke 24:37

They were startled and frightened, thinking they saw a **ghost**.

Luke 24:39

"Look at my hands and my feet. It is I myself! Touch me and see; a **ghost** does not have flesh and bones, as you see I have."

As you can see by these verses, ghosts are very much a recognized entity within the Biblical text. If ghosts do not exist, why are they mentioned and acknowledged in the Bible? By this act of acknowledgment, their collective name becomes a truism. The word *ghost* is also taken and used as an adjective in the word *ghostlike*, so it supersedes the word in noun form. The Contemporary English Version (CEV) Bible also uses the term "ghost-town" in several places. This is used to describe deserted buildings and homes. It may not be a direct reference to the origin of the phrase, but may be used to highlight where only ghosts now dwell or haunt devoid of the living. But again it would suggest that ghosts are considered to exist when the Bible uses the word *ghost* as a descriptive word.

Jeremiah 22:6

Listen to what I think about it:

The palace of Judah's king is as glorious as Gilead or Lebanon's highest peaks. But it will be as empty as a ghost-town when I'm through with it.

Ezekiel 26:19

I, the Lord God, will turn you into a ghost-town.

Hebrews is an early sermon that exhorts Christians to persevere in the face of persecution. In this text it mentions that spirits and ghosts are all around us. We are told that Abraham, Isaac, Jacob and the rest of the Old Testament believers had the faith to look into the future and believe the Messiah would come. The reference to the cloud of witnesses is the acknowledgement that the ghosts of those that paved the way before us are now seeing the proof of their faith.

Hebrews 12:1
Therefore, since we are surrounded by such a great cloud of witnesses, let us throw off everything that hinders and the sin that so easily entangles. And let us run with perseverance the race marked out for us.

Jesus himself made a statement about not being a ghost. He was thus stating that ghosts do exist but that He was not one of them. So apparitions and ghosts were believed to be real by the followers of Jesus who were learning rapidly from Him about the spirit realm. Others outside of Jesus' teaching circle were also aware of the concept of ghosts during Jesus' time on earth. Ghosts appeared in the city of Jerusalem after Jesus' resurrection.

Matthew 27:52-53
...and the tombs were opened, and many bodies of the saints who have fallen asleep, arose; and having come forth out of the tombs after Jesus' rising, they went into the holy city and appeared to many.

Research reveals that ghost stories from this period existed outside of the Bible, so people of this time were well aware of such concepts; the Roman historian and senator Tacitus (A.D. 56-117) wrote of ghostly encounters, as did the Roman letter writer Pliny the Younger (A.D. 61-115).

The text of the Bible confirms that the spirit and physical realms do co-exist with one another, but on different planes. It is a spiritual truth that what exists here on earth must first exist in the spirit realm. The Bible proclaims this idea directly in the very first part of the Lord's Prayer:

On earth, (the physical realm) as it is (first) in heaven (the realm of spirit).

This sentence also reinforces our claims that reincarnation is possible if we started in heaven in spirit and then came back to earth in a physical form.

So what does the Bible tell us is a ghost? The word ghost can be found in several different instances within the Biblical text. First, it is used in the King James Bible to describe the Holy Ghost; next, it is mentioned as being the physical apparition of a spirit; and finally, it is used in the phrase *to give up the ghost*, meaning to die, in other words, to let the ghost out of the body upon death. The following three extracts are taken from the King James Bible.

Genesis 25:8
Then Abraham gave up the ghost, and died in a good old age, an old man, and full of years; and was gathered to his people.

John 19:30
When Jesus therefore had received the vinegar, he said, It is finished: and he bowed his head, and gave up the ghost.

Job 14:10
But man dieth, and wasteth away: yea, man giveth up the ghost, and where is he?

These passages describe situations in which the action of physical dying involves letting out the spirit inside of us which can then go forth as a ghost. In Hebrew, the words in these verses literally translate as *gave up the ghost*, meaning to breathe out, to be dead and perish in the physical sense. It is interesting that man should breathe out his spirit as it was God that breathed spirit into man. Thus, when a man dies, his spirit returns to God—or dies in hell.

Jesus is actually our main teacher when discussing ghosts. Jesus tells us that ghosts do not have bodies, thus proving that He is real and not a ghost. From His very lips we learn that ghosts are real and are the spirits of dead people (as His disciples believed Him to be dead) with no physical body. Jesus actually appeared to several people after his resurrection, including Simon and Mary Magdalene. He appeared to two of his followers in a different form but was nevertheless recognizable to them.

Luke 24:34

...and saying, "It is true! The Lord has risen and has appeared to Simon."

Mark 16:9

When Jesus rose early on the first day of the week, he appeared first to Mary Magdalene, out of whom he had driven seven demons.

Mark 16:12

Afterward Jesus appeared in a different form to two of them while they were walking in the country.

The term "appeared" would indicate that He manifested Himself from the invisible to the visible, just as a ghost might manifest itself from the spirit world to the physical realm.

Jesus also appeared to the remaining eleven disciples and stood in their midst during their conversation, having been manifested from the spirit realm. Jesus made himself known to them in a miraculous manner to assure the disciples of His peace.

Luke 24:36

While they were still talking about this, Jesus himself stood among them and said to them, "Peace be with you."

Luke 24:39

Look at my hands and my feet. It is I myself! Touch me and see; a ghost does not have flesh and bones, as you see I have.

Jesus was in fact proclaiming that he was not a ghost because he had flesh and bone. But Jesus was becoming visible in the same manner that a ghost would; flesh and bone does not just appear out of thin air. It is possible, of course, for ghosts to manifest physical attributes so they can turn lights on and off, slam doors, create the noise of footsteps, and mess around with your faucet. A physicist will tell you that energy is required to undertake these activities and this energy is believed to be electrical magnetic field (EMF) energy. It is noticeable that meters and equipment that read EMF give very high readings before and after ghosts have manifested themselves or where paranormal activity has occurred.

Note that the disciples become afraid of Jesus after He appeared before their eyes. This also happened when Jesus walked on the water toward His disciples who were in a boat. This suggests that they had a knowledge of ghost-like behavior.

Matthew 14:25-27
Shortly before dawn Jesus went out to them, walking on the lake. When the disciples saw him walking on the lake, they were terrified. "It's a ghost," they said, and cried out in fear. But Jesus immediately said to them: "Take courage! It is I. Don't be afraid."

Mark 6:48-50
He saw the disciples straining at the oars, because the wind was against them. Shortly before dawn he went out to them, walking on the lake. He was about to pass by them, [49] but when they saw him walking on the lake, they thought he was a ghost. They cried out, [50] because they all saw him and were terrified. Immediately he spoke to them and said, "Take courage! It is I. Don't be afraid."

John 6:19-20
When they had rowed about three or four miles, they saw Jesus approaching the boat, walking on the water; and they

were frightened. [20] But he said to them, "It is I; don't be afraid."

Luke 24:39
"Look at my hands and my feet. It is I myself! Touch me and see; a ghost does not have flesh and bones, as you see I have."

The Christians that wish to admonish what we do often point to a particular Bible passage to illustrate what they believe is a haunting—a man possessed by a legion of demons residing in a graveyard in Gerasenes (Mark 5:1-20). This is used as an example of Satan's power to deceive man about ghosts. But the text clearly states that the man in question was actually alive, so he could not have been in spirit. He just happened to be in a graveyard, probably to get some peace away from an emotionally frenzied community. Graveyards during this time were placed on the edges of towns beyond the encircling protective walls, so the spirits could not disturb the living. This, of course, is further indication that people of this period had knowledge of what ghosts were.

The passage in Mark relates the case of a living person being controlled by demons to terrorize the people of that area. Dark forces will do anything within their power to deceive people, to lead people away from God and to make you believe ghosts do not exist, as this is the proof of everlasting life through God. I believe, through my experiences and studies, that if you see your recently deceased mother, and hear or feel the message she wants to impart, then that is exactly what she is doing.

So are all of our deceased relatives and friends demons in disguise? Conservative-thinking Christians would say yes. Even from a fundamentalist point of view, however, this is statistically impossible. Let us start by looking at some basic facts. There were only a set number of angels created, not an infinite number. We know this because Revelation states:

Revelation 12:4
His tail drew a third of the stars of heaven and threw them to the earth.

The term *stars* in this text is in reference to angels, so if we know that Satan took a third of them down to earth (fallen angels), then there must be a countable number. You can only take a third if you know how many there were to start with. The exact number of angels that were created varies depending on what part of the Bible you are reading.

Jude 1:14
Enoch, the seventh from Adam, prophesied about them: "See, the Lord is coming with thousands upon thousands of his holy ones".

Hebrews 12:22
But you have come to Mount Zion, to the city of the living God, the heavenly Jerusalem. You have come to thousands upon thousands of angels in joyful assembly.

Revelation 5:11
Then I looked and heard the voice of many angels, numbering thousands upon thousands, and ten thousand times ten thousand. They encircled the throne and the living creatures and the elders.

Daniel 7:10
Thousands upon thousands attended him; ten thousand times ten thousand stood before him.

So Daniel puts the figure at *ten thousand times ten thousand*. If we take this as the largest Biblically documented number (100 million), we can assume that a third of those angels are fallen (have become demons) as previously discussed. That equates to 33,333,333 fallen angels. This is a significantly limited amount considering that since this Biblical event vast numbers of demons have been exorcised and sent back to their realm.

The late Pope John Paul II personally performed three exorcisms during his reign and Father Gabriele Amorth, the Church's chief exorcist, claims to have expelled more than 300 demons a year from the confines of his Vatican office. As of 2015, there are some 350 exorcists operating on behalf of the Catholic Church in just Italy alone. So we can surmise that the original assumed number of fallen angels can be significantly lowered. If Father Gabriele Amorth removes 300 a year and there are 350 exorcists working in Italy and if each of them also removed 300 demons a year on average, we are left with a figure of 105,300 exorcisms a year. This means you can remove and send back every demon ever created in just 316 years in Italy alone. And we have been exorcising demons all over the world for millennia!

Statistically, then, the chance of any human being ever confronting a demon is limited. That is not to say we must ignore them or not protect ourselves during our readings, investigations and healing. But we must have realistic thoughts about their commonality and influence. For the few demons that remain, I am sure they have more important things to do than dress as a dead relative and appear in your kitchen at three a.m. when you are going to the fridge for a snack. Whatever the number of demons, the point remains that there just aren't very many. I have investigated many haunted buildings and locations all over the world in the last fifteen years and I believe I have only come across a handful of demons. They are incredibly rare. During your lifetime it is unlikely that you will ever encounter one.

Satan and his minions are working to mislead us and turn us away from the Gospel. But they work cleverly. They may not be solely working on us individually, but on the big corporations that sell Ouija boards in the children's section of the multinational grocery stores, or the news agencies that peddle falsehoods and hyperbole. It is what we absorb, what we see, what we are exposed to. It is important to remember that if we have God by our side, then we have no need to fear any entity or spirit whether it has evil intentions or not. From our pulpits we often hear that good will always overcome evil and that the word of God will always scatter darkness; so why is it, then, that many of these same clergy tell their parishioners they need to be afraid of a demonic force pretending to be a deceased relative?

It is easy to see why those without knowledge or experience would label every encounter they hear about, or witness with a ghost or spirit, as an interaction with a dark entity. It is a kneejerk reflex that closes down any further questioning or dialogue. This response will elicit fear and it will end the conversation in its tracks with those who have many questions and confusion. Those who attend church will have fear placed in their path and will not be allowed to discuss the incident further, in their eyes giving Satan and his minions the "energy of recognition." Nobody wants to then admit that Satan has visited their house and property, and has tried to communicate with them. Such experiences of naturally occurring ghost encounters with pleasant reasonable people in spirit, are now falsely seen as an experience that has a sense of shame, embarrassment and fear about it, as if it is an indication or measure of how good a Christian you are.

Many people have the genuine concern of being ostracized from their religious community—a fear of ridicule, loss of social standing and respect, even castigation for not being a true Christian. Remember that North Carolina, Arkansas, Maryland, Mississippi, South Carolina, Tennessee and Texas all ban atheists from holding public office. So not being accepted within the church community can have far-reaching consequences.

Certainly the church cannot easily admit the true answers to the questions they are asked about the paranormal because those questions are beyond their knowledge of current science and contemporary thinking. The local pastor or minister will have little or no experience of the paranormal world. They are not engaging with spirits or investigating the paranormal world on a daily basis, as I am. This approach to difficult questions about unknown phenomena can be traced through the history of the church over the last six hundred years.

I found in my studies of the early Italian Renaissance period a policy of the church to repress and subjugate the population on paranormal issues they cannot provide answers for. This era is littered with flying saucers (UFOs) in paintings, placed there at the request of the Catholic Church. The *Madonna and Child with the Infant St. John* attributed to Sebatiano Mainardi in the late 15th century, and the *Glorification of the Eucharist* by Bonaventura Salimbeni in 1600 are two famous examples. This I believe was in part due to the local peasantry asking the clergy what the strange flying objects were that they would see occasionally in the skies as they worked in the fields. Without having an answer, the perfect response would have been that these objects were angels or the work of God. Subsequently, flying objects resembling those observed were included in the backgrounds of paintings and frescos to reinforce the answer. This is a very good way to repress any kind of fear of the unknown, and also enables the clergy to form an acceptable answer to a question they have no answer for.

Let us now proceed to the next question—can we talk to ghosts? We have already established through the Biblical text that ghosts exist, so what does the word of God say about interaction with ghosts? The following text reinforces the fact that ghosts are real, but more importantly it shows that we can share a dialogue with them. These verses can be found in the famous Mount of Transfiguration passage. In these accounts, Jesus and three of His apostles proceed to a mountain. Jesus then begins to emit bright rays of light. Then the dead prophets Moses and Elijah appear and speak with Jesus as witnessed by his disciples.

Mark 9:4
And there appeared before them Elijah and Moses, who were talking with Jesus.

Matthew 17:3
Just then there appeared before them Moses and Elijah,
talking with Jesus.

Luke 9:30
Two men, Moses and Elijah, appeared in glorious splendor,
talking with Jesus.

The following verses confirm that spirits appear to the living
but also teach us another very important spiritual truth—that Jesus
spoke with people from the other side of the grave. Therefore, those
on the other side can speak to us, and we can speak to them! Jesus,
whom we are told is to be our example, showed us that spirits will
communicate with us.

Matthew 22:32
"'I am the God of Abraham, the God of Isaac, and the God of
Jacob'? He is not the God of the dead but of the living."

Mark 12:27
He is not the God of the dead, but of the living. You are badly
mistaken!

Luke 20:38
"He is not the God of the dead, but of the living, for to him all
are alive."

We are aware that any communication with the spirit world
is frowned upon as an unChristian act, yet Jesus felt it important
enough to reveal to us what was really going on behind the scenes.
If one were to take the familiar saying "What would Jesus do?" the
answer would be that He would speak with ghosts. Jesus actually
asked his apostles to come with Him to witness this.

Mark 9:2
After six days Jesus took Peter, James and John with him and

led them up a high mountain, where they were all alone. There he was transfigured before them.

Matthew 17:1
After six days Jesus took with him Peter, James and John the brother of James, and led them up a high mountain by themselves.

Luke 9:28
About eight days after Jesus said this, he took Peter, John and James with him and went up onto a mountain to pray.

Jesus seemed to understand what was going on behind the veil of the physical world. Perhaps we should follow His example and not fear ghosts, but rather seek to understand the truth of our relationships with them in the spirit realm. I initially found it remarkable that my own experiences of talking with ghosts were reflected perfectly in the Bible. The descriptions of how ghosts were engaged with by Jesus and others, and how they looked, read like a documentary for me. This would suggest that people's experiences of this paranormal phenomena have been the same throughout history.

The most prominent ghost story in the Bible that involves a dialogue was described in 1 Samuel. King Saul was preparing to do battle against the Philistines, but the Lord had departed from him. Saul wanted to get a prediction on the outcome of the battle, so he decided to consult a medium at Endor to call up the spirit of Samuel the prophet. Many theologians believe that God intervened and caused Samuel's spirit to manifest itself to Saul. If this was in fact the case, then we have the perfect example of how God works with psychics and mediums to provide a manifestation. Here is the story:

1 Samuel 28:3-20
Now Samuel was dead, and all Israel had mourned for him and buried him in his own town of Ramah. Saul had expelled the mediums and spiritists from the land.

⁴The Philistines assembled and came and set up camp at Shunem, while Saul gathered all Israel and set up camp at Gilboa. ⁵When Saul saw the Philistine army, he was afraid; terror filled his heart. ⁶He inquired of the LORD, BUT THE LORD DID NOT ANSWER HIM BY DREAMS OR URIM OR PROPHETS. ⁷Saul then said to his attendants, "Find me a woman who is a medium, so I may go and inquire of her."

"There is one in Endor," they said.

⁸So Saul disguised himself, putting on other clothes, and at night he and two men went to the woman. "Consult a spirit for me," he said, "and bring up for me the one I name."

⁹But the woman said to him, "Surely you know what Saul has done. He has cut off the mediums and spiritists from the land. Why have you set a trap for my life to bring about my death?"

¹⁰Saul swore to her by the LORD, "AS SURELY AS THE LORD LIVES, YOU WILL NOT BE PUNISHED FOR THIS."

¹¹Then the woman asked, "Whom shall I bring up for you?"

"Bring up Samuel," he said.

¹²When the woman saw Samuel, she cried out at the top of her voice and said to Saul, "Why have you deceived me? You are Saul!"

¹³The king said to her, "Don't be afraid. What do you see?"

The woman said, "I see a ghostly figure coming up out of the earth."

¹⁴"What does he look like?" he asked.

"An old man wearing a robe is coming up," she said.

Then Saul knew it was Samuel, and he bowed down and prostrated himself with his face to the ground.

¹⁵ Samuel said to Saul, "Why have you disturbed me by bringing me up?"

"I am in great distress," Saul said. "The Philistines are fighting against me, and God has departed from me. He no longer answers me, either by prophets or by dreams. So I have called on you to tell me what to do."

¹⁶ Samuel said, "Why do you consult me, now that the Lord has departed frm you and become your enemy? ⁷ The Lord hs done what he predicted through me. The Lord hs torn the Kingdom out of your hands and given it to one of your neighbors—to David. ¹⁸ Because you did not obey the Lord or carry out his fierce wratth against the Amalekites, the Lord has done this to you today. ¹⁹ The Lord will deliver both Israel and you into the hands of the Philistines, and tomorrow you and your sons will be with me. The Lord will also give the army of Israel into the hands of the Philistines."

²⁰ Immediately Saul fell full length on the ground, filled with fear because of Samuel's words. His strength was gone, for he had eaten nothing all that day and all that night.

Saul expelled all mediums and spiritists from the land for practicing under the auspices of other gods. But he tried to engage with the Lord himself for the information he was seeking through the very practices he outlawed, thus showing that it was acceptable to contact and engage with the Lord in this manner. Saul took this step because the Lord did not answer him by the usual means of dreams, urim (divination) or prophets. This also indicates that Saul was used to communicating with the Lord through divination and clairvoyance, practices he was familiar with and apparently used successfully over a period of time.

Interestingly, the female medium who conjures up the ghost is not admonished for facilitating the dialogue between the spirit of Samuel and Saul. One would think that God would punish the woman if her behavior was wrong, but punishment is never mentioned. The concern was why Saul never went directly to God. The actual dialogue is free from criticism, even though it was not what Saul wanted to hear.

The following sentence is also from the text of 1 Samuel and is very important in reflecting our thoughts and ideas. It suggests that Samuel was occupied in an activity in the afterlife as he claims to have been disturbed when Saul interrupts him.

1 Samuel 28:15
Samuel said to Saul, "Why have you disturbed me by bringing me up?"

I have already explained that spirits engage in the activities they enjoyed when they were in the physical realm, but they do not work in an employed sense for financial reward. It states in Ecclesiastes that those in spirits will not work and it is true in the spirit world that no money is exchanged for labor and those that are undertaking work are doing so for the love of the job, or out of a sense of loyalty or a convention set in place during their own physical lifetime of subservience.

Ecclesiastes 9:10
Whatever your hand finds to do, do it with all your might, for in the realm of the dead, where you are going, there is neither working nor planning nor knowledge nor wisdom.

It is also interesting that Samuel told Saul that he had *brought him up*, suggesting that he had come from a place lower or below. This idea is also reflected in Job where it is written that *one who goes down to the grave does not return.*

Job 7:9-10
As a cloud vanishes and is gone, so one who goes down to the grave does not return. 10 He will never come to his house again; his place will know him no more.

Certainly this statement is true. If you perceive *going down to the grave* to be a metaphor for *going down to hell*, then as we know, no return is possible. If the phrase *go down to the grave* simply means to leave this physical realm, then again we know that we can't return in the same physical form as before, and we have already touched upon our existence being lost to the knowledge of man.

I believe that the non-returnable aspect of being dead in spirit is then one of the consequences of hell; thus, you will receive no opportunity of a return to the physical realm to gain knowledge of your family.

Job 14:21
If their children are honored, they do not know it; if their offspring are brought low, they do not see it.

The Bible often refers to spirits as *familiar spirits*, as in an intimate or personal association, or one well acquainted. This suggests that those we were close to in life can be with us again in the spirit realm. This is true of my own personal experiences of accessing the spirit world as previously mentioned.

I have explained that I am taken to the individuals in spirit that I wish to engage with via God. But the following passages give us warning of having this communication and interaction with familiar spirits outside of God.

Leviticus 19:31
Do not turn to mediums or seek out spiritists, for you will be defiled by them. I am the Lord your God.

Deuteronomy 18:11
...or casts spells, or who is a medium or spiritist or who consults the dead.

Isaiah 8:19
When someone tells you to consult mediums and spiritists, who whisper and mutter, should not a people inquire of their God? Why consult the dead on behalf of the living?

These statements can now be placed in the context of not contacting and talking to spirits unless through God, as opposed to the pagan gods. This was the historical context placed on these directives. We are also now aware that when it tells us to not consult the dead on behalf of the living, we are talking about those dead in spirit—those sent to hell after judgment. Remember, we are accessing those that have eternal life.

So what are the ways we can talk to ghosts and spirits? Considering what we have learned so far, it seems that a verbal dialogue is the best way to proceed, in order to have a normal kind of conversation. The words you speak need to be audible within the room for the ghost to access them. If the person next to you cannot hear your voice then the ghost will not hear it either. Remember that we should show respect at all times (these are heavenly spirits after all). Antagonizing people even in the spirit world would not be following Christian ideals. They are people's relatives and loved ones. Talk to them in a way that you would want others to talk to your grandmother.

A second way of communicating is through thoughts and impressions (as a clairvoyant would proceed). Remember that we must be vigilant against the ways of Satan in all that we do, so make sure you protect yourself and others, taking the precautions outlined in the chapter on prayer and my writing on protection.

I would never ever touch the Ouija board as a device to communicate with the spirit world, and I would advise the same for you; the process of using a spirit board requires you to ask a spirit to come into you as a means of providing the information required. This leaves you open to all kinds of beings and entities coming to reside in you, without any kind of filter or discernment. The use of contemporary devices such as digital voice recorders and ghost boxes are just tools to improve the possibility of a dialogue, and unlike the Ouija board, you are asking for spirits to communicate via the equipment rather than through you.

I have never experienced a situation where a person has told me they used the Ouija board and as a result have a fabulous life. In all the years I have hosted paranormal radio shows I have found myself having to deal with a considerable number of listeners who have engaged with the Ouija board, and their lives were subsequently ruined as a result. They had health issues, they had lost their jobs, their partners, their money, and had experienced all manner of personal misadventures and ill-fortune as a result.

It is also worth considering the concept of whether we should perform the process of *crossing-over* when dealing with a ghost or spirit. This is the idea that ghosts and spirits can be trapped on this earthly realm unable or unwilling to move into the spirit world. This is perceived to be because the spirit has missed the concept of a door to the light, a momentary portal that allows us in spirit to begin our journey to heaven. It is believed that a spirit may refuse to access this portal because they are worried they may be judged, especially if they believe they have led an immoral life, or they did not take the opportunity presented to them due to an obligation they felt they needed to achieve first, or to perhaps deliver a message. Other spirits may not even be aware they are dead, especially if their death was unexpected or sudden. So they are confused perhaps and unaware of where they are and their circumstances.

It is then expected in some people's thinking to perform a ritual or ceremony to facilitate the *crossing-over* of a spirit from this world to the spirit realm. This is believed to be achieved through a dialogue with the spirit in terms of counselling or cajoling, or through the summoning of angels to help guide the spirit into the light. Other practices can involve an eclectic mix of techniques ranging from smudging to the use of salt or blessed oil.

The concept of *crossing-over* in my eyes is problematic though, and I wish for you to consider the following. If God chose to end the physical life of a person, and if God has now chosen not to embrace them into his land yet, that is His choice. Remember we are not to question His thoughts and motives. So if we cross them into His land we could be in conflict with God's will. I have very rarely found an individual in spirit to be trapped though. So this is not a conclusion you should jump to when engaging with any spirit.

Spirits are normally just visiting and can go back and forth between this physical realm and the spirit realm without any issue. And those that are perceived to be trapped are normally avoiding the natural process of moving into the spirit realm due to the fear of being judged. I find it difficult to believe that a quick and unexpected death can lead to a spirit being disorientated and unsure of their current predicament for any length of time. The concept of progressing into the light is very firmly entrenched into our culture as a convention, and I am sure that it would not take long for the recently deceased individual to work out what has happened to them, unless a sense of denial is prevalent.

Please also be aware that just because a spirit or ghost claims to be a lost small child, does not mean it is actually a lost small child. It may be disguising and presenting itself as that in order to play with our motives and responses, to gain favor and sympathy. On no account ask that spirit to come home with you! Remember also that there is a delineation between the process of *crossing-over* when solely concerned with deceased people in spirit, and the banishment and removal of dark and demonic entities.

Many years ago I witnessed a paranormal investigation that tried to facilitate the *crossing-over* of a spirit. This was deemed to be successful at the time. When I returned later that year I discovered the same spirit to be back. I genuinely believe that God had put them back to where He wanted them to be in the first place. This interference may only serve to make Him unhappy.

We are now aware that ghosts and spirits do exist and that through the teaching of Jesus it is reasonable to engage with them in conversation. Yet parts of the Bible continue to remind us that the spirits of deceased humans inhabit only one of two places, heaven or hell; this would suggest that there should be no such thing as a haunting on earth. To answer this let us look at what actually happens to us when we finally leave this physical realm—what the Bible says happens when our spirit leaves the body and the journey it undertakes. Here, in the epistle to the Hebrews in the New Testament, we are told that we are to face a judgment in spirit based on our design for life in the physical realm.

Hebrews 9:27

Just as people are destined to die once, and after that to face judgment,

The Bible proceeds to reinforce this concept in Revelation and not only states again that we will be judged, but that a record is documented in a book.

Revelation 20:11-15

Then I saw a great white throne and him who was seated on it. The earth and the heavens fled from his presence, and there was no place for them. [12] And I saw the dead, great and small, standing before the throne, and books were opened. Another book was opened, which is the book of life. The dead were judged according to what they had done as recorded in the books. [13] The sea gave up the dead that were in it, and death and Hades gave up the dead that were in them, and each person was judged according to what they had done. [14] Then death and Hades were thrown into the lake of fire. The lake of fire is the second death. [15] Anyone whose name was not found written in the book of life was thrown into the lake of fire.

Paul highlights in Corinthians that the result of a believer's spirit leaving a person's physical body is being at home with the Lord. The term *at home* is an interesting phrase because it suggests a familiarity, in that we are returning as if we have been there before. This is further recognition of the concept of previous lives and that we may have frequented heaven previously, as well as the sense of comfort and safeness associated with the term *at home*.

2 Corinthians 5:6-8

Therefore we are always confident and know that as long as we are at home in the body we are away from the Lord. [7] For we live by faith, not by sight. [8] We are confident, I say, and would prefer to be away from the body and at home with the Lord.

Philippians 1:23
I am torn between the two: I desire to depart and be with Christ, which is better by far;

As Paul has already told us, coming back home to God in spirit is only reserved for believers, those with faith. In the passage below Matthew also reinforces this concept.

Matthew 25:46
"Then they will go away to eternal punishment, but the righteous to eternal life."

The prophet Isaiah proclaims that the righteous are not concerned about passing because they know that they will be taken into God's embrace, to be spared from the instruments of evil in hell.

Isaiah 57:1
The righteous perish, and no one takes it to heart; the devout are taken away, and no one understands that the righteous are taken away to be spared from evil.

Due to compassion, the righteous are taken away when they perish, that they may not see the evil, nor share in it, nor be tempted by it. The righteous man, when he dies, enters into peace and rest. The unrighteous that are sent to hell will die in spirit and face the agonies and torment of fire. This vision of hell is perfectly illustrated in the following text of Luke in the story of the rich man and the poor man.

Luke 16:22-24
"The time came when the beggar died and the angels carried him to Abraham's side. The rich man also died and was buried. [23] In Hades, where he was in torment, he looked up and saw Abraham far away, with Lazarus by his side. [24] So he called to him, 'Father Abraham, have pity on me and send Lazarus to dip the tip of his finger in water and cool my tongue, because I am in agony in this fire.'"

We are further told in both Ezekiel and 2 Thessalonians that those who sin will go to hell.

Ezekiel 18:4

For everyone belongs to me, the parent as well as the child—both alike belong to me. The one who sins is the one who will die.

2 Thessalonians 2:9-10

The coming of the lawless one will be in accordance with how Satan works. He will use all sorts of displays of power through signs and wonders that serve the lie, [10] and all the ways that wickedness deceives those who are perishing. They perish because they refused to love the truth and so be saved.

All of the passages above tell us that there is no in-between, no middle ground between heaven and hell. This means that there should in theory be no possibility of remaining on earth in the form of a spirit or a ghost. So let's scrutinize then what a haunting actually is.

"Residual" and "intelligent" are the two main categories for hauntings, although others, like the energy of a poltergeist haunting, also exist. A "residual haunting" is like a footprint pressed into the fabric of history. It is the replaying of an event and will allow no interaction with the ghost or spirit, like a theater production where an actor walks onto a stage at 8 p.m. every night and replays a set of actions and words. An "intelligent haunting" is when we can interact with the ghost or spirit to have a stimulus and response dialogue. The Bible actually describes in various places what it is to be in spirit and what we can and can't achieve when we are physically dead, as explained in Ecclesiastes.

Ecclesiastes 9:5-10

For the living know that they will die, but the dead know nothing; they have no further reward, and even their name is forgotten. [6] Their love, their hate and their jealousy have long since vanished; never again will they have a part in anything that happens under the sun.

[7] Go, eat your food with gladness, and drink your wine with a joyful heart, for God has already approved what you do. [8] Always be clothed in white, and always anoint your head with oil. [9] Enjoy life with your wife, whom you love, all the days of this meaningless life that God has given you under the sun—all your meaningless days. For this is your lot in life and in your toilsome labor under the sun. [10] Whatever your hand finds to do, do it with all your might, for in the realm of the dead, where you are going, there is neither working nor planning nor knowledge nor wisdom.

Let's analyze this text to gain an understanding of its meaning: *For the living know that they will die*, is a constant truth, as we all know our physical existence will one day end. We cannot deny this; one day we will all die in this realm. This is stated in Psalm 49.

Psalm 49:10
For all can see that the wise die, that the foolish and the senseless also perish, leaving their wealth to others.

But the dead know nothing refers to those dead in hell, as we have already established. Thus they will have no knowledge as they fail to exist. *They have no further reward*; there is no further reward because they have been judged and the reward (if they are righteous) has already been given via the passage into heaven. The phrase *and even their name is forgotten* tells us that many of their names have been lost to the knowledge of man over time. This is a reflection of people's preoccupations and a lack of importance placed on history. The website ancestry.com conducted a survey of Americans in 2007 and found that only 43 percent of adults knew both their grandmothers' maiden names; and a further 22 percent did not know what their grandfathers had done for a living.

Ecclesiastes proceeds to say that *their love, their hate and their jealousy have long since vanished.* If the spirits of those that have left the physical realm are rewarded with everything they desire in heaven, then those aspects will obviously no longer exist. The statement that says...*never again will they have a part in anything that happens under the sun* just explains that they are literally no longer under the sun—they are in heaven.

The phrase *for in the realm of the dead, where you are going, there is neither working nor planning nor knowledge nor wisdom* is also true—no working, no planning, and no knowledge of the future or insights into tomorrow. This has certainly been my experience when talking to those in spirit, although, as previously discussed, many choose to continue to work because that is what they enjoyed doing when they were in the physical realm. But it was for the love of the task than for any financial reward.

In the Psalm below we can see this concept outlined further when it discusses plans in the physical realm coming to nothing when you pass into the spirit realm.

Psalm 146:3-4

Do not put your trust in princes, in human beings, who cannot save.⁴When their spirit departs, they return to the ground; on that very day their plans come to nothing.

This verse illustrates that if you are fixing a car in the physical world and you then pass into spirit your car is not going to be fixed. It is however possible to have a spirit engage with a person in the physical realm to help a person finish a project, acting as a kind of muse, by stating ideas and appearing in dreams. This though is reliant on the physical person acting as a go-between to oversee what the spirit is requesting, and the spirit cannot engage with those projects without that third party interaction.

We have discussed that only the spirits of those who sin die and go to hell. The rest reside in heaven as described in Isaiah.

Isaiah 26:14

They are now dead, they live no more; their spirits do not rise. You punished them and brought them to ruin; you wiped out all memory of them.

So when we are talking to ghosts and not just viewing them like a looped recording, we are either accessing those that are in heaven or those that are in hell. And we already know that those in hell are dead and we should not be accessing them anyway. So let us take a deeper look at the concepts of hell and heaven.

You may be surprised to know that there is not a single mention of hell in the Old Testament, and the word is only mentioned thirteen times in the New Testament. If it were not for the writings of Matthew and Mark it would only be worthy of three mentions.

Matthew 5:22

But I tell you that anyone who is angry with a brother or sister will be subject to judgment. Again, anyone who says to a brother or sister, 'Raca,' is answerable to the court. And anyone who says, 'You fool!' will be in danger of the fire of **hell**.

Matthew 5:29

If your right eye causes you to stumble, gouge it out and throw it away. It is better for you to lose one part of your body than for your whole body to be thrown into **hell**.

Matthew 5:30

And if your right hand causes you to stumble, cut it off and throw it away. It is better for you to lose one part of your body than for your whole body to go into **hell**.

Matthew 10:28

Do not be afraid of those who kill the body but cannot kill the soul. Rather, be afraid of the One who can destroy both soul and body in **hell**.

Matthew 18:9
And if your eye causes you to stumble, gouge it out and throw it away. It is better for you to enter life with one eye than to have two eyes and be thrown into the fire of **hell**.

Matthew 23:15
"Woe to you, teachers of the law and Pharisees, you hypocrites! You travel over land and sea to win a single convert, and when you have succeeded, you make them twice as much a child of **hell** as you are."

Matthew 23:33

"You snakes! You brood of vipers! How will you escape being condemned to **hell**?"

Mark 9:43
If your hand causes you to stumble, cut it off. It is better for you to enter life maimed than with two hands to go into **hell**, where the fire never goes out.

Mark 9:45
And if your foot causes you to stumble, cut it off. It is better for you to enter life crippled than to have two feet and be thrown into **hell**.

Mark 9:47
And if your eye causes you to stumble, pluck it out. It is better for you to enter the kingdom of God with one eye than to have two eyes and be thrown into **hell**...

Luke 12:5
But I will show you whom you should fear: Fear him who, after your body has been killed, has authority to throw you into **hell**. Yes, I tell you, fear him.

James 3:6
The tongue also is a fire, a world of evil among the parts of the body. It corrupts the whole body, sets the whole course of one's life on fire, and is itself set on fire by **hell**.

2 Peter 2:4
For if God did not spare angels when they sinned, but sent them to **hell**, putting them in chains of darkness to be held for judgment.

What we have learned from these limited glimpses is that hell has imprisoning darkness inhabited by fallen angels. There is fire, and it contains the dead spirits of those that have sinned. The Christian doctrine of hell is also called by several other names such as the Hebrew word Gehenna. Gehenna is a term derived from a valley on the outskirts of Jerusalem known as the Valley of the Son of Hinnom. This location was where the child sacrifices took place for the pagan gods that are admonished by our Lord in the Bible. Thus it was considered to be cursed and the destination of the wicked. We have already seen that the criticism the Lord has of mediums and spiritists was due to their association with pagan gods. The King James Version of the Bible and the NIV Bible also directly translate Gehenna into the word hell. The Greek word Hades is mentioned just eight times in the NIV translation of the Bible and does not provide us with any more information than we already have.

We know that spirits die in hell and there is a non-returnable permanence about your spirit dying and of the effects of burning and destruction. So by default that only leaves the spirits that are in heaven. This is shown in the passage from Psalm 49 below.

Psalms 49:17-19
...for they will take nothing with them when they die, their splendor will not descend with them. [18] Though while they live they count themselves blessed— and people praise you

when you prosper—[19] they will join those who have gone before them, who will never again see the light of life.

This text also discusses the idea that you cannot take anything with you in spirit. Other cultures that leave precious items, weapons, and even slaves and warriors—like the Egyptians with their pyramid-encased funerary—are admonished by God for their belief in pagan gods. Even today in this physical realm you see individuals being buried with their Cadillacs or motorcycles. Some ghosts even choose to haunt properties like gold mines, or look to protect a house they once lived in that is now being remodeled. They cannot take it with them, but that does not stop them from trying or coming back in spirit to place a watchful eye over proceedings.

I have in my career managed to access spirits that I personally would have thought to be impossible to contact, due to the belief that I considered their actions to be worthy of being sent to hell. I remember a reading I was asked to do for a client who wanted to contact her deceased father. The contents of that reading could distress the client. Her father came through straight away and I described him to her perfectly, a tall upright man with a full dark brown beard and a disposition of being quietly brooding. He was also dressed in a naval uniform and was standing on the deck of a naval vessel, like a destroyer. I mentioned that he looked like a career naval man. She acknowledged that this was her father and she proceeded to ask if he was sorry for what he had done. I focused back on her father who had heard her statement. I received the words that he was not sorry at all, without knowing at that stage what he should be sorry for.

It has been my experience that many clients wish to open a dialogue with a spirit so they can have a sense of apology or closure with that individual. It is painful to have to tell some clients that the spirit they are trying to communicate with is still the same person with the same flaws and inadequacies. When I tell the client the disparaging or cutting remarks an individual in spirit wishes me to relay to them, it shows that the essence of that person is still there. Of course, I could say to my client that the spirit *does* love them and *does* miss them, when the spirit has not expressed such sentiments. But this would be an untruth. When I communicate exactly what the spirit is relating, the client usually responds by telling me that is exactly what the spirit would have said had he or she physically been present.

I was then told by my client that her father had actually raped her when she was a baby, as well as other infant members of her family. I considered this despicable act and how the spirit of her father had then presented himself. I know that sinners are supposed to go to hell and I know we cannot access spirits that are in hell because they have been killed. So how was I able to access a child rapist? Surely hell is reserved for people just like that. I thought about this reading long and hard and I realized that this spirit was all alone on the ship, a ship that appeared to be drifting and was ultimately not going anywhere. This struck me as a punishment if this is what he has to endure for an eternity. It is interesting to then consider again Revelation 20:14 when we are told that only at the end of days will sinners be cast into hell. This is the second death in spirit after the first death that is the physical body. This is telling us that hell is currently un-resided.

Revelation 20:14
Then death and Hades were thrown into the lake of fire. The lake of fire is the second death.

It does intrigue me as to who actually goes to hell based on this experience. I have also spoken to many spirits over the years who had committed suicide. It is not uncommon for clients to come and see me who are worried that their loved ones may have been cast into hell because they committed suicide and are then looking for a reassurance that they are safe in spirit. This false fear has been manifested by some terrible and quite frankly shocking rhetoric that I have heard coming from religious leaders when talking to freshly grieving relatives. I have always managed to contact every suicide victim I was asked to contact, and on every occasion they were in spirit and happy. I believe based on these experiences that God is a forgiving and loving God and that suicide comes from a place of mental illness in the shape of depression and desperation. And an illness is not considered to be punishable by God. Would God stop you from entering into his Eternal Embrace if an illness like cancer or heart disease removed you from this physical realm?

This would support my own personal view that only fallen angels are vanquished to hell at the present time. The individual on the ship was either in a limbo period of purgatory or he was choosing to punish himself. Purgatory would then perhaps be as simple as standing in a never-ending line at a grocery store sandwiched between a screaming child and a teenager playing overly loud music through their headphones. This sense of waiting may be why spirits are notoriously difficult to contact directly after they have passed from the physical realm. I normally would require a client to wait at least a month before we talk to the spirit. This is also to give my client the opportunity to progress past the first stages of grieving.

Based on my experience, I do not believe heaven to be a place of entrapment; it is not a one way trip. I have seen and spoken thousands of times to spirits that reside in heaven, but are back visiting in this realm to watch over a new grandchild or family wedding, or to check on what a new family has done with the house they used to live in. I believe spirits that reside in heaven can come and go as they please. So a haunting is either a residual footprint of a replayed event, in which the spirit is not present and cannot be interacted with, or it is an "intelligent haunting" in which the spirit is visiting from heaven and can engage with contact during its stay.

I am constantly asked why ghosts and spirits visiting from heaven would want to hang out in miserable attics or damp basements, and why dirty, wet, dark environments are frequented by entities if they can walk through walls and go anywhere. Why would anyone want to leave paradise to spend time in such places? The fact is that paranormal investigation teams have beckoned them there. The spirits have come to where they have been invited. They may have been wandering around quite happily in a salubrious part of a hotel, where they once visited or worked, and then were asked to come and say hello. So the spirits work their way down to the dark basement where the investigation is taking place, or they become interested in what is going on down there. They would have actually come to any part of the building where the vigil was taking place.

It is also worth remembering that as beings of energy that spirits may be best suited to communicating and displaying acts of physicality in environments where there is as a catalyst for this to happen. Energy and electricity is better suited to damp wet locations as it conducts and travels better as compared to a dry location. It may not be that graveyards, basements and castles are more haunted, they just might be the dampest and the wettest places. So we may have a better opportunity to interact with spirits in these types of surroundings.

It is also recognized that if investigations are taking place in a public building, like a city hall or library, or a building with a lot of foot traffic, like a hotel or bar for example, that the basement or attic may be the only place that noise pollution does not affect the highly sensitive recording equipment used to document the paranormal activity. I can also say that if the energy of a spirit is emitting a faint glow of light, like an orb of energy, it can be seen much easier against a dark background, as opposed to a bright environment where it would go unnoticed. A dark environment also heightens our sense of smell, touch and hearing.

I am also asked why ghosts only come out at night. The answer is—they don't. But paranormal teams investigate at night due to the nature of when team members are available and when the properties can be accessed, so many more encounters happen during these times. You could easily walk through a grocery store during the day and have a ghost walk right by you without even realizing it. I once witnessed the ghost of an old lady in a black shawl with a weather-worn deep-lined face looking at me from no more than touching distance, in the middle of a field in bright sunshine during the middle of the day. Rod Serling of *The Twilight Zone* once said that "There is nothing in the dark that isn't there when the lights are on."

Ghosts and spirits are obviously a reflection of what a person was like when they had a physical form. It has been my experience that when I am called to investigate a haunted building, that the owner wants to jump to the worst case scenario, labelling the activity in their home or work place as demonic. Their eagerness to take the incidents they are experiencing to the most extreme of conclusions is because of fear and a lack of understanding—a fear that is fed by television entertainment shows and misinformation delivered by uninformed church clergy where we are led to believe that darkness lurks on every corner. Yet we have already shown that demonic entities are limited in number.

I have investigated some of the most haunted buildings all over the world for the last twenty years, and I could count on the fingers of one hand when an entity has proven to be demonic and non-human. The key here is to remember that if you are a rude, inconsiderate, intolerant, recidivist when you were alive, then you will be the same when you are dead. Thankfully, despite what the media would have you believe, most people are polite, well-meaning and pleasant.

If you are experiencing the light switches being turned on or off, if you are hearing footsteps, doors slamming, or the faucet being manipulated, then someone is trying to gain your attention. It would be a good idea to then work out who that individual is. I have already spoken about the ability of ghosts and spirits to be able to move freely from heaven to this physical realm. So why would they want to occupy your abode? I would suggest that they are perhaps a deceased member of your family or a departed friend that wishes to relay a message to you in order to help your grieving process. Remember that when they die you are just grieving over them, but they are grieving over everybody they have left behind. It could also be that the spirit used to work in or own the property at some point in the past, and they are checking to see what changes you have made.

Demonic entities have little time for messing around with your faucet. They will generally want to reside in areas of disease, conflict, war, fear, famine, death and suffering. The energy provided by these scenarios will act like a finger buffet of darkness in order to make them more powerful. In your average day, in your average house, in your average town, they would have little or no reason to interfere with your life. This does not mean that we are not careful and do not protect ourselves and our environment, but their threat of a presence does need to be considered and put into perspective.

I have actually experienced these dark forces when I have investigated and visited buildings that look to induce fear, like the Halloween house destinations that spring up in the fall with tableaus designed to scare the visitor for the thrill of being frightened. The location itself may not be haunted and may not have a history of paranormal activity or incidents surrounding deaths or accidents. But darkness will seek to feed on the fear that is left in the energy of the property by those that have paid for the experience.

It is also true that I have experienced dark human spirits literally attached to or standing next to individuals in a bar. It makes perfect sense that if a spirit was an alcoholic or drug abuser in their physical lifetime, then they would want to keep close to a similar person that is still in the physical existence, especially if that individual is also an alcoholic or a drug user. The spirit wants to feel that same high once again and can only do so by coming into that physical body. We have all seen that guy slumped over the bar all alone in a funky cloud of darkness. A darker non-human entity may have taken that individual to that place of addiction and depression, but other spirits with questionable integrity can take advantage of the situation.

Using logic, I can suggest that only good spirits go to heaven and only these spirits are the ones that can visit us and observe the physical realm. I can still currently contact the bad spirits, but they appear to be in a place of purgatory and limbo, and are ultimately waiting for the second death, this time in spirit, as highlighted in Revelation. Remember that a grumpy, upset, frustrated, or angry spirit, does not make it by default Biblically evil.

Prophets and Psychics

I have found it very difficult to differentiate between prophets and psychics. I would suggest, however, that a psychic should not pronounce himself or herself to be a prophet. That should be for the church to decide. Read the following and ask yourself whether the dictionary definition is describing a prophet (accepted and embraced by the church) or a psychic (denounced and rejected by some individuals within the church).

> One who utters inspired revelations: one gifted with more than ordinary spiritual and moral insight; one who foretells future events – a predictor, marked by an extraordinary sensitivity, perception, or understanding.

The fact that one cannot easily delineate between the two by a dictionary definition suggests their sameness. Intrinsically, the difference appears to be based on where the individual is getting their source material. If knowledge gained is from God or through His will, the individual is a prophet; if it is through other means, the individual is considered to be psychic: simply put *one who utters Divinely inspired spiritual revelations and one who utters spiritually inspired revelations.* So it would now suggest that the words prophet and psychic are interchangeable if their source material is the same and both are working through God. So let us study the role of the prophet within the Bible.

J. Barton Payne's *Encyclopedia of Biblical Prophecy* lists 1,239 prophecies in the Old Testament and 578 prophecies in the New Testament, for a total of 1,817. These encompass 8,352 verses. So my question is: if God was worried about the work of psychics, why did He employ so many psychics throughout the Bible (especially before Christ) to convey his own words, messages and thoughts to mankind?

Hebrews 1:1-2
In the past God spoke to our ancestors through the prophets at many times and in various ways,

² but in these last days he has spoken to us by his Son, whom he appointed heir of all things, and through whom also he made the universe.

The book of Hebrews was written to show the ultimate supremacy of Jesus and has a very powerful and dramatic opening passage. In one paragraph the reader is transported from the familiarity of the Old Testament into the New Testament age in which Christ is now the ultimate seat of power in the universe; the superiority of Jesus over all rival claims to allegiance which His readers were feeling and hearing.

What is also presented to us is the acknowledgment that God used prophets to communicate his messages to man before the time of Christ. So God would hardly be denigrating the work of a prophet/psychic if he was using them so freely and frequently. God's enthusiasm to employ such methods becomes more intriguing when we consider that He has a readymade army of angels to call upon to undertake such tasks already. After all, angels were created solely for this purpose. The word angel derives from the old English and Germanic word *engel* and the French word *angele*. Both come from the Latin *angelus,* which in turn is the Romanization of the ancient Greek word *angelos*, all meaning messenger.

In the following passage from Kings we have an example of a prophetic visit God paid to Solomon and the communion he had with God, which placed a greater honor upon Solomon than all the wealth and power of his kingdom.

1 Kings 3:5
At Gibeon the Lord appeared to Solomon during the night in a dream, and God said, "Ask for whatever you want me to give you."

Including Solomon, I counted at least 73 different prophets used by God, from Aaron (Exodus 7:1) through to Zephaniah (Zephaniah 1:1). I included only those individuals who were clearly defined as prophets in the Bible either by explicit statement or by strong contextual implication. Fifteen more were individuals who were recorded as having had visionary or prophetic experiences but had no history of any major or consistent prophetic calling. What this means is that the prophets used in the Bible are receiving knowledge, guidance and information about future events through God's intervention via direct messages, visions, dreams and visitations. I am sure that even more prophets were used by God, but their prophecies were never written down. We are also still discovering ancient texts and many more documents that had been lost to man that contain new prophets and prophecies.

Moses was very much aware of the importance of prophets in delivering the word of God or, in this context, Jesus.

Acts 3:22-23
For Moses said, 'The Lord your God will raise up for you a prophet like me from among your own people; you must listen to everything he tells you. 23 Anyone who does not listen to him will be completely cut off from their people."

This verse seems harsh in its tone and brings to mind intolerant individuals who wish to excommunicate those who go against their teaching.

A good example of an interaction between God and a prophet comes from the story of Nathan and King David's plan to build a temple. Nathan was a prophet during the reign of King David. He is a central character in three key recorded stories, two in the book of 2 Samuel and a third in the book of 1 Kings.

King David had just brought the Ark of God to Jerusalem. King David's plan was to build a house for God. David shared his plan with Nathan who boldly gave his support to the project. Following Nathan's words of support, the Lord gave a revelation to Nathan that put David's role into perspective. David would have rest from his enemies and the long-promised Messiah would come from the house of David. However, David was not to build the temple. Nathan reported this entire revelation back to King David. Here is the story:

1 Chronicles 17:1-15

After David was settled in his palace, he said to Nathan the prophet, "Here I am, living in a house of cedar, while the ark of the covenant of the LORD IS UNDER A TENT."

[2] Nathan replied to David, "Whatever you have in mind, do it, for God is with you."

[3] But that night the word of God came to Nathan, saying:

[4] "Go and tell my servant David, 'This is what the Lord says: You are not the one to buld me a house to dwell in. [5] I have not dwelt in a house from the day I brought Israel up out of Egypt to this day. I have moved from one tent site to another, from one dwelling place to another. [6] Wherever I have moved with all the Israelites, did I ever say to any of their leaders whom I commanded to shepherd my people, "Why have you not built me a house of cedar?"'

[7] "Now then, tell my servant David, 'This is what the Lord Almighty says: I took you from the pasture, from tending the flock, and appointed you ruler over my people Israel. [8] I have been with you wherever you have gone, and I have cut off all your enemies from before you. Now I will make your name like

the names of the greatest men on earth. [9] And I will provide a place for my people Israel and will plant them so that they can have a home of their own and no longer be disturbed. Wicked people will not oppress them anymore, as they did at the beginning [10] and have done ever since the time I appointed leaders over my people Israel. I will also subdue all your enemies.'"

"'I declare to you that the LORD WILL BUILD A HOUSE FOR YOU: [11] When your days are over and you go to be with your ancestors, I will raise up your offspring to succeed you, one of your own sons, and I will establish his kingdom. [12] He is the one who will build a house for me, and I will establish his throne forever. [13] I will be his father, and he will be my son. I will never take my love away from him, as I took it away from your predecessor. [14] I will set him over my house and my kingdom forever; his throne will be established forever.'"

[15] Nathan reported to David all the words of this entire revelation.

Nathan's prophecy encouraged King David to go ahead and build a temple of God. Unfortunately, this was not what God had planned. Note that critics of psychics should find it interesting that God did not reject Nathan for his erroneous prophecy; He continued to use Nathan to correct the matter by informing him of the true message. This is an important text, as God not only allowed Nathan to be wrong in his prophecy, but also corrected him without admonishment.

The following quote affirms that the skill of prophecy does exist and is God-given; it also states that at any time God can take it away again if he sees fit to do so. Paul is making reference to a time when these skills will ultimately cease and not be required because something better will replace them.

1 Corinthians 13:8-10

Love never fails. But where there are prophecies, they will cease; where there are tongues, they will be stilled; where there is knowledge, it will pass away.

[9] For we know in part and we prophesy in part, [10] but when completeness comes, what is in part disappears.

Those who take an opposing view might argue that the time has already come to cease these skills as the truth has now been given and there is no need to continue the revelation. They might suggest that the *spiritual gifts* discussed both before and after this were deemed temporary, as they were given to us by God for a specific purpose. The New Testament did not exist during the apostolic era and the miraculous gifts confirmed the message, guided the recording of the message, and allowed communications between people speaking in different languages. This writing was aimed at the fledgling church at a time when the scriptures were still being documented. Once those scriptures were finished, it was argued that the gifts had then served their purpose in guiding the apostles, along with the prophets, teachers, and those upon whom the apostles had laid hands. I would remind those thinkers that our skills are only with us because God allows us to have them. If a cessation was required by God, I am sure he would have removed them by now. I also believe that prophets exist now to deal with the ever changing world.

Additionally, many parts of earth are still yet to be touched by God's hand, so missionary work and the teachings of Christianity are still necessary practices. Language also remains a barrier to dialogue and communication worldwide. When we are finally in a position to say the whole world has been shown the glory of the gospel, and when we speak solely in one tongue (literally), then you may expect those gifts to cease. The argument that prophecy is no longer needed is clearly wrong, there is still very much a need.

The Bible also tells us to be aware of false prophets that can provide us with tainted information and misguided hopes, potentially ruining our lives, future plans and dreams, and those of our clients.

Matthew 24:24

For false messiahs and false prophets will appear and perform great signs and wonders to deceive, if possible, even the elect.

The false prophets described in Matthew are not only the prophets that promote mass-suicides and murder, but also those that promote false messages and embrace financial gain and fame over the true word of the Gospel. Peter states below that the truth of Christian redemption is held in contempt by many because of the immoral behavior of professing Christians. The primary motive behind such false teaching as discussed is greed and ego. They do not hesitate to take hurtful advantage of their followers in order to enrich themselves. They exploit by deceit.

2 Peter 2:1-3

But there were also false prophets among the people, just as there will be false teachers among you. They will secretly introduce destructive heresies, even denying the sovereign Lord who bought them —bringing swift destruction on themselves. ² Many will follow their depraved conduct and will bring the way of truth into disrepute. ³ In their greed these teachers will exploit you with fabricated stories. Their condemnation has long been hanging over them, and their destruction has not been sleeping.

Peter is delineating between the false prophets (and prophecies) of the past who looked to distort Christian teaching, compared to the apostles of his time that are working correctly through God but are still admonished by false teachers. This resonates perfectly with the climate of today as we have previously discussed, with the opposition the psychic and healer receives from some individuals within the church.

Paul returns to the basics in the verse below to try and keep the church on track. He is looking to respond to the influences of false teaching, stating that the foundation of any church depends on the practice and faith of its leaders. This instruction also applies to all Christians as we must all strive be a model of God's teaching.

1 Timothy 4:1-4

The Spirit clearly says that in later times some will abandon the faith and follow deceiving spirits and things taught by demons. [2] Such teachings come through hypocritical liars, whose consciences have been seared as with a hot iron. [3] They forbid people to marry and order them to abstain from certain foods, which God created to be received with thanksgiving by those who believe and who know the truth. [4] For everything God created is good, and nothing is to be rejected if it is received with thanksgiving, [5] because it is consecrated by the word of God and prayer.

The text in Deuteronomy is God's way of saying that those who work outside of his teachings are false prophets because the information they receive could be influenced by Satan's hand.

Deuteronomy 18:20

But a prophet who presumes to speak in my name anything I have not commanded, or a prophet who speaks in the name of other gods, is to be put to death.

The key here is that we don't know for sure one way or the other whether Satan is involved. For example, the following text denigrates divination through astrology.

Isaiah 47:13-15

All the counsel you have received has only worn you out! Let your astrologers come forward, those stargazers who make predictions month by month, let them save you from what is coming upon you.

[14] Surely they are like stubble; the fire will burn them up. They cannot even save themselves from the power of the flame. These are not coals for warmth; this is not a fire to sit by.

¹⁵ That is all they are to you—these you have dealt with and labored with since childhood. All of them go on in their error; there is not one that can save you.

The reference above to monthly astrology readings refers to the reports astronomers were required to send in every month to King Belshazzar. The last two verses are commenting on those that practice in the black arts outside of God's word and they will not be around when they are needed. In simple terms, we must remember that the planets are named after Roman pagan gods—so this represents a process of bypassing God and His divine wisdom by looking at divination through pagan Gods.

The Bible warns us further that working outside of God's love and teachings will result in having the possible influence of Satan running through our work. In the following Corinthians passage, we are told that feasting is part of the heathen sacrifice of worshipping the idol to whom it was made and having fellowship or communion with it. This is denying Christianity because communion with Christ and communion with the Devil cannot both be embraced together. If Christians venture into places and join in sacrifices to the lust of the flesh, the lust of the eye, and the pride of life, they will provoke God.

1 Corinthians 10:20
...but the sacrifices of pagans are offered to demons, not to God, and I do not want you to be participants with demons.

Many individuals within the church also label psychics as false prophets because no matter how much evidence we provide from the Bible, their minds are set. It is easier to attack than to search and become knowledgeable, and then to respond with an informed opinion. The following sentence in Revelation provides very powerful imagery. It describes metaphorically the words and thoughts of impure spirits spewing forth from the lips of the prophet who is working outside of God.

Revelations 16:13

Then I saw three impure spirits that looked like frogs; they came out of the mouth of the dragon, out of the mouth of the beast and out of the mouth of the false prophet.

We are further warned in Jeremiah's letter below that God sees which prophets are working with Him and which are only saying they work with Him in a bid to mislead the people.

Jeremiah 29:8-9

Yes, this is what the Lord Almighty, the God of Israel, says: "Do not let the prophets and diviners among you deceive you. Do not listen to the dreams you encourage them to have. [9] They are prophesying lies to you in my name. I have not sent them," declares the Lord.

There is a responsibility here for the client to research and question with whom the psychic is working. Many clients wish to be deceived. They are desperately looking for answers from anybody about their life choices and their grieving processes. They are then falling prey to unscrupulous individuals. The first century Roman satirist Petronius said, "The world wants to be deceived, so let it be deceived." It is not just credulity that misleads people, but their own love of darkness over the light. It is not a passive process to go and access a psychic or healer. It is not like taking antibiotics—you have a responsibility to God and yourself. This lack of questioning and blind following is shown perfectly with the example and story of Aaron and the golden calf in Exodus 32:1-4.

In John we are cautioned further to not believe or trust every spirit that is in communication through those that pretend to be with the Spirit of God. We are told there were real communications from the Divine Spirit, so regrettably others have then pretended to have the same dialogue. John tells us that others may be so evil and so impudent as to pretend the same, and they are not to be believed. Although it is open to abuses, God has sent psychics and teachers into the world and has given us supernatural revelations. God does however give a test whereby the disciples may try these pretending spirits. We are to scrutinize and examine the claims of these false prophets to see whether they be of God. It should not seem strange to us that false teachers and psychics set themselves up in today's society and the church, because it was also clearly the case in the apostles' time. Unfortunately, what they are doing is allowing Satan to have his way prepared and his rise facilitated by the spirit of error and deception in the minds of men. This has been foretold.

1 John 4:1-4

Dear friends, do not believe every spirit, but test the spirits to see whether they are from God, because many false prophets have gone out into the world. [2] This is how you can recognize the Spirit of God: Every spirit that acknowledges that Jesus Christ has come in the flesh is from God, [3] but every spirit that does not acknowledge Jesus is not from God. This is the spirit of the antichrist, which you have heard is coming and even now is already in the world.

[4] You, dear children, are from God and have overcome them, because the one who is in you is greater than the one who is in the world.

In my experience of visiting, working and lecturing at psychic expos, and in interviewing psychics on my radio show over the years, I have come across many that I believe to be unethical in many respects. Some are making up the information they believe they are receiving. Others falsely tell clients they are going to die or that they have a demonic entity with them. I have even witnessed one trying to solicit money from clients for fictitious business ventures during actual readings. The Bible text provides us with information on how to spot and acknowledge false spirits as well as false prophets. Here are some guidelines to help you and others to recognize true intentions.

Matthew 7:15-20
Watch out for false prophets. They come to you in sheep's clothing, but inwardly they are ferocious wolves. [16] By their fruit you will recognize them. Do people pick grapes from thorn bushes, or figs from thistles? [17] Likewise, every good tree bears good fruit, but a bad tree bears bad fruit. [18] A good tree cannot bear bad fruit, and a bad tree cannot bear good fruit. [19] Every tree that does not bear good fruit is cut down and thrown into the fire. [20] Thus, by their fruit you will recognize them.

Matthew clearly states that you must look at what intentions healers and psychics have and what backgrounds they possess. It tells us that it is not necessarily the outcome or *the fruits*, but from *where the fruits were picked*. The passages below highlight what these fruits are and from what trees they are taken. They also highlight the differences between ourselves and the false prophets.

Galatians 5:22-23
But the fruit of the Spirit is love, joy, peace, forbearance, kindness, goodness, faithfulness, [23] gentleness and self-control. Against such things there is no law.

John 13:35
"By this everyone will know that you are my disciples, if you love one another."

Job 1:8
Then the Lord said to Satan, "Have you considered my servant Job? There is no one on earth like him; he is blameless and upright, a man who fears God and shuns evil."

So, we can be recognized by our fruits—the way we present ourselves to others; our design for life; the way we treat others; our morals and scruples; through the undertaking of loving and giving, being righteous without ego or a sense of self adulation; and being blameless and upright in our practices and how we engage with others and earth. We must see ourselves as servants of God in the same way you would not want to embarrass your parents through your own behavior. Of course, as human beings we are incapable of living a saintly life without sin. To quote Pablo Picasso, *every act of creation is first an act of destruction,* but it is all about your intensions. Remember that Jesus died on the cross for our sins. He has already taken into account the things we do in our lives that we are not proud of—our moments of fallibility. Remember, none of us are without sin. This is reinforced in the familiar verse below in John.

John 8:7
So when they continued asking him, he lifted up himself, and said unto them, He that is without sin among you, let him first cast a stone at her.

The Bible says that we will have God's power over pagan practices, as evident by the text below, which describes how Aaron's staff becomes a snake. This suggests that by working through the Christian faith and its doctrines we make ourselves more powerful and affective, placing us in a better position to help others who seek our skills.

Exodus 7:8-12
The Lord said to Moses and Aaron, [9] "When Pharaoh says to you, 'Perform a miracle,' then say to Aaron, 'Take your staff and throw it down before Pharaoh,' and it will become a snake."

[10] So Moses and Aaron went to Pharaoh and did just as the Lord commanded. Aaron threw his staff down in front of Pharaoh and his officials, and it became a snake. [11] Pharaoh then summoned wise men and sorcerers, and the Egyptian magicians also did the same things by their secret arts: [12] Each one threw down his staff and it became a snake. But Aaron's staff swallowed up their staffs.

Let me remind you that we are not here to judge or criticize. How would that make us any different than those that criticize us? This text is not meant to be judgmental, it is opinion based on what the Bible is telling us. This book is solely about people who possess psychic gifts and how we practice mediumship and healing as Christians in the name of God. Individuals can do whatever they wish. But we need to be informed if we are to make decisions based on religion in conjunction with the practice of psychic abilities.

The verse below highlights this way of thinking. It speaks about Christians who are weak in faith. It teaches us that we should not look down on, or scorn, judge or shun those that are not strong in faith. We should love them as Christ would. It gives context to the love Christ had for them by his own sacrifice of dying for them. Christ cautions his disciples about despising their fellow disciples as little and below them, especially since so much notice and care was taken of them, both in heaven and on earth.

Matthew 18:10
See that you do not despise one of these little ones. For I tell you that their angels in heaven always see the face of my Father in heaven.

Revelation 20:10
And the devil, who deceived them, was thrown into the lake of burning sulfur, where the beast and the false prophet had been thrown. They will be tormented day and night for ever and ever.

In Revelation we are told that false prophets are seen in the same context as the Devil. It states that they will be cast into hell where we are now aware they will die in spirit. Conveniently, the Bible actually gives us in 1 John a list of rules on how to discriminate between spirits that come with the Lord's blessing and those that are a conjuring of Satan's hand.

1 John 4:1-6

Dear friends, do not believe every spirit, but test the spirits to see whether they are from God, because many false prophets have gone out into the world.

[2] This is how you can recognize the Spirit of God: Every spirit that acknowledges that Jesus Christ has come in the flesh is from God,

[3] but every spirit that does not acknowledge Jesus is not from God. This is the spirit of the antichrist, which you have heard is coming and even now is already in the world.

[4] You, dear children, are from God and have overcome them, because the one who is in you is greater than the one who is in the world.

[5] They are from the world and therefore speak from the viewpoint of the world, and the world listens to them.

[6] We are from God, and whoever knows God listens to us; but whoever is not from God does not listen to us. This is how we recognize the Spirit of truth and the spirit of falsehood.

We have discussed that the terms "prophet" and "psychic" are almost interchangeable in terms of what skills both possess. And we are aware that God employed prophets to relay His messages to man through visions, dreams, voices and visitations. We have also covered how to make sure your own practice is acceptable to God and how we can identify a false psychic/prophet. If you believe someone to be a false prophet, then it is wise to remember that you are not meant to take any action against that individual; that is God's job and you must be aware that only He has the power to ultimately judge if necessary. You need to focus on you and your life and rest in the knowledge that everyone else will have their day of judgment too.

Prayer

In this chapter I will cover how to pray and what to pray for in the context of a psychic and healer. As firmly stated in Thessalonians below, being a Christian requires you to pray, and pray regularly.

1 Thessalonians 5:17
Pray continually...

So what is prayer? Various forms of prayer appear in the Bible, the most common forms being petition, thanksgiving and worship. The longest book in the Bible is the book of Psalms, 150 religious songs that are often regarded as prayers. So let me start by saying that prayer is not a letter to Santa, or is it a wish list that includes a red Corvette and the winning lottery ticket. To me it is stating one's gratitude of God, Jesus Christ and the Holy Spirit.

Colossians 1:3
We always thank God, the Father of our Lord Jesus Christ, when we pray for you,

I also give thanks for the world, breaking it down into people, places, things and events. It is asking for help with your life, having a successful meeting, a safe drive, or a positive health check. It is asking for help to be sent to those in need—people who are sick, depressed, or in a traumatic or stressful situation. Importantly, we must add our intention to receive the gift and tools to be psychic and to heal. Lastly, we must also listen. This is a two way process as God may wish to communicate with us. There needs to be an acceptance that our own unique skills and gifts are God-given and that worshipping through prayer will help to ensure that those gifts remain sharp and intact. If God decides in his wisdom to ever remove them, so be it. Then our paths will lead in other directions.

We are required to give ourselves fully and believe without question or doubt that our prayers are heard in heaven. This is confirmed in 2 Chronicles.

2 Chronicles 7:14

If my people, who are called by my name, will humble themselves and pray and seek my face and turn from their wicked ways, then will I hear from heaven and will forgive their sin and will heal their land.

To undertake the process of prayer with a wholehearted attitude our heart must be in God; proof does not come from great miracles or signs but by intent and by the implementing of Christian values. This manifesto is reinforced through the text of Jeremiah.

Jeremiah 29:13

You will seek me and find me when you seek me with all your heart.

If we work without pride and remain obedient and true to God's words, then we shall receive. Jeremiah also tells us that when we seek the Lord we will always find Him. He is a God hearing prayer and granting us His presence when we seek Him with eagerness and desire, with integrity and sincerity and a true heart.

According to the promise in the following passage from 1 John, what we receive is entirely owing to His own grace and favor and for the sake of Christ; but keeping the commands of God is a necessary adjunct in asking.

1 John 3:22
And receive from him anything we ask, because we keep his commands and do what pleases him.

Any sense of wavering in this belief will ultimately result in our failure to receive. So faith and belief are intrinsic to all we do in prayer. This directive is reinforced in both the texts of James, Mark and John below.

James 1:6-7
But when you ask, you must believe and not doubt, because the one who doubts is like a wave of the sea, blown and tossed by the wind.

[7] That person should not expect to receive anything from the Lord.

Mark 11:24
Therefore I tell you, whatever you ask for in prayer, believe that you have received it, and it will be yours.

John 11:40
Then Jesus said, "Did I not tell you that if you believe, you will see the glory of God?"

It must be mentioned that God will decide what we receive and when. We must have faith, as the verses above state, that what we ask for is heard. Remember though that God does not wear a wristwatch, so we are not in control of when it happens. If God does not give what we ask for on our schedule, it is because He knows we do not need it, or that it is not for our own good.

It is also important to remain righteous, acting in an upright manner and conforming to a standard of morality and virtue. A righteous person can be trusted to act honorably regardless of the circumstances. This, of course, is very different from the term *self-righteous*, where one is smugly moralistic and intolerant of the opinions and behavior of others.

Psalms 92:12

The righteous will flourish like a palm tree, they will grow like a cedar of Lebanon.

The following passages are about being ethical, decent, reliable, honest and true in your work and how you present yourself and behave to the client and the public as a whole.

Luke 9:24

For whoever wants to save their life will lose it, but whoever loses their life for me will save it.

James 5:20

Remember this: Whoever turns a sinner from the error of their way will save them from death and cover over a multitude of sins.

There is an old saying: *going to church does not make you a Christian any more than going to the garage makes you a car.* Christianity is about how you live your life, rather than the reflex of putting in a few hours on a Sunday to keep yourself in credit. You would do well to think of life as a proving ground that solely determines the outcome of who will go to heaven or hell. It clearly states in Galatians that those who embrace a non-Christian design for life in terms of their morality will not be welcomed into God's embrace, even if we state we are Christian in name.

Galatians 5:19-23

The acts of the flesh are obvious: sexual immorality, impurity and debauchery; [20] idolatry and witchcraft; hatred, discord, jealousy, fits of rage, selfish ambition, dissensions, factions [21] and envy; drunkenness, orgies, and the like. I warn you, as I did before, that those who live like this will not inherit the kingdom of God.

[22] But the fruit of the Spirit is love, joy, peace, forbearance, kindness, goodness, faithfulness, [23] gentleness and self-control. Against such things there is no law.

Your Christian practice as a healer will only be fruitful if you pray to God and live a righteous life. Then you will become powerful and effective in this field.

James 5:16
Therefore confess your sins to each other and pray for each other so that you may be healed. The prayer of a righteous man is powerful and effective.

It is important to realize that you cannot fool God and that you cannot just outwardly project what you believe to be the demeanor of a Christian. It needs to run through everything you do and be intrinsic to your very fiber and being.

Matthew 7:21-23
"Not everyone who says to me, 'Lord, Lord,' will enter the kingdom of heaven, but only the one who does the will of my Father who is in heaven.

[22] Many will say to me on that day, 'Lord, Lord, did we not prophesy in your name and in your name drive out demons and in your name perform many miracles?'

[23] Then I will tell them plainly, 'I never knew you. Away from me, you evildoers!'"

During his Sermon on the Mount Jesus states in Matthew (above) that many are fooling themselves by calling themselves Christians, but have never followed Jesus. This is reinforced when Jesus tells us the following in the same verse.

Matthew 7:18
A good tree cannot bear bad fruit, and a bad tree cannot bear good fruit.

Jesus taught so much about the kingdom of God being one of relationship and rightness with God. It's not about prophesying and casting out demons. It's about love and your relationship with God and each other.

So what are we asking for? Prayer for us is multi-layered. We are thankful to God for our gifts and we ask Him to continue to bless us with them. And we are seeking protection. Satan will want to pollute our readings and cause disharmony and discord. It is the prayer aspect before and during our work that takes us out of the mire of sorcery and away from the clutches of Satan. Otherwise our work of being psychic and healing would not be undertaken in God's name. This warning is highlighted in 1 Timothy.

1 Timothy 4:1
The Spirit clearly says that in later times some will abandon the faith and follow deceiving spirits and things taught by demons.

We are ensuring that Satan does not interfere with our processes, and we are not giving heed to deceiving spirits. This is most important because a misheard message or a false sentence could move your client down a completely different path, one that could lead to darkness. A scenario in which a well-meaning client is asking her father in spirit whether she should sell the family farm could place that individual on two very different paths toward an outcome of hearing a "yes" or a "no."

We must be aware of how Satan can affect our work and misguide us causing torment and pain of others, even if we do not feel Satan's presence or are ignorant of his plans. We are warned of how Satan can lead us astray in Revelation.

Revelation 12:9
The great dragon was hurled down—that ancient serpent called the devil, or Satan, who leads the whole world astray. He was hurled to the earth, and his angels with him.

The awareness that this is possible if we are not guarded and do not protect ourselves properly through Christian ceremony, as already discussed, is key. Vigilance and prayer is our armor.

Matthew 26:41
"Watch and pray so that you will not fall into temptation. The spirit is willing, but the flesh is weak."

If we are aware of Satan's schemes we are taking the power he has over our work away. Paul, in the following passage from 2 Corinthians, uses the word *schemes* or *devices* from the translation of the Greek word *noema*. The same Greek word also has the meaning of *thoughts* or *mind*.

2 Corinthians 2:11
In order that Satan might not outwit us. For we are not unaware of his schemes.

The NIV translation misses the wordplay here. The Greek translation is literally, "We are not unmindful of his mind," which in the case of Satan is a scheming, plotting mind. Paul is thinking of how Satan can take advantage of the discipline process to alienate a person from the church or even from Christianity. This is a perfect example of how the church can react to our practices of being psychic and healing. Paul is describing how Satan can take advantage of an unforgiving clergy and congregation to sow division and dissension in the church.

Paul's objective is to take captive of every thought solely for the obedience to Christ as we can see in 2 Corinthians. We live in a time where the mind is deemphasized and the needs of the individual are elevated, where everybody is concerned and preoccupied in oneself, to the detriment of others. In contrast to this way of thinking, Paul affirms that the mind matters. Indeed, it is so crucial that he focuses all of his efforts on taking every thought captive and making it obey Christ. Christ must reign supreme in our minds over our individual wants and needs.

2 Corinthians 10:5
We demolish arguments and every pretension that sets itself up against the knowledge of God, and we take captive every thought to make it obedient to Christ.

Satan and his followers are liars intent on spreading confusion, fear, and a distrust of God. Remember that a lie is anything that contradicts the truth. God's word is the truth. We are warned of this in the passage of John 8.

John 8:44
You belong to your father, the devil, and you want to carry out your father's desires. He was a murderer from the beginning, not holding to the truth, for there is no truth in him. When he lies, he speaks his native language, for he is a liar and the father of lies.

Jesus tells it like it really is. In this text he reveals that the devil himself is the real spiritual father of those that are unbelieving. Satan was a murderer from the beginning, indirectly murdering Adam and Eve and then Abel through Cain. And we must guard against following suit by desiring to murder Jesus himself. The devil does not dwell in or possess any truth, and when the devil lies he speaks his true nature and character. Satan is the originator of lies and his children will follow suit with their own lies.

Satan and his demons will constantly try to give us thoughts by which to control us. He has the power to put thoughts into our minds at any time when we are working. Remember that Satan can also disguise himself as a useful spirit in a ruse or deception. In John, and through the writings of Paul, we are told if we foster this awareness and work diligently, we can identify those implanted thoughts and evil spirits and take them captive by the power of God's living words residing in our hearts.

Prayer is a very personal process and I prefer to use the prayers I have constructed for myself and my own use. They come from the heart and anything I create is through God and so will fulfill the criteria I am using them for. We have been given direction on how to pray and what to pray for and we are told that we should pray often. It is intrinsic to everything we do as Christians. Remember though that if you are not looking to receive or are blind to receiving, then God can give you everything you have wished for, yet it can pass you by without even being recognized or seen. Use every minute of every day as a moment to consider or reflect on whether this was your moment to receive from God. Then reach out your hand and grab onto it tightly before it disappears. Learning to receive is in many respects more important than learning to ask.

Protection and the Removal of Darkness

On our journey towards understanding how to be a practicing Christian psychic, we must first learn to protect ourselves, otherwise we will not ascend beyond the blindness I have previously discussed. In this chapter I will outline the concept of protection and the different ways we can keep ourselves safe from dark influences during our work. I will highlight how to remove dark energies, beings and spirits from people and properties.

Satan and his minions will do everything in their power to convince society that psychics and healers are working with them. So society will be persuaded in this deceit to not to be healed, comforted and helped. This idea can be cleverly reinforced if it is introduced to people by those that masquerade as servants of righteousness, as Paul outlines in Corinthians.

2 Corinthians 11:14-15
And no wonder, for Satan himself masquerades as an angel of light. [15] It is not surprising, then, if his servants also masquerade as servants of righteousness. Their end will be what their actions deserve.

So safety and precaution must be intrinsic to all we do, although we can ultimately remove this threat successfully through our faith and by engaging in prayer.

Ephesians 6:11-12
Put on the whole armor of God, that ye may be able to stand against the wiles of the devil. For we wrestle not against flesh and blood, but against principalities, against powers, against the rulers of the darkness of this world, against spiritual wickedness in high places.

In many of the passages in this epistle Paul states the opposition the Christian has against a heathen lifestyle, and the duty of rebuking and putting to shame the works of darkness. But here in Ephesians he warns us that the struggle is not a struggle with the flesh and blood of wicked men, but a war with the spiritual powers of evil. He tells us the armor given to us is God, our protector, in all its completeness, providing full protection against all the wiles (the stratagems of a skillful leader) of Satan. Hence its completeness corresponds to the divine perfection of His true humanity; to receive and use His salvation and wield the spiritual energy of His Word.

Our struggle is with the hand-to-hand battle we undertake with these evil spirits, a personal grapple with the darkest foe. It is a real power, but limited and transitory, able only to enslave those who yield themselves to it and are destined to be overcome. Paul tells us that the power of evil is attacking in spirit in a higher aspect than just in this the physical realm. Those who believe psychics and healers partner with dark forces will do well to remember the following: we have the power over Satan to render him impotent, and we should implement this on a regular basis. The following verses highlight how faith in God and the word of the Bible will always defeat darkness and evil.

Luke 10:19
I have given you authority to trample on snakes and scorpions and to overcome all the power of the enemy; nothing will harm you.

Romans 8:31
What, then, shall we say in response to these things? If God is for us, who can be against us?

James 4:7-8
Submit yourselves, then, to God. Resist the devil, and he will flee from you.

[8] Come near to God and he will come near to you. Wash your hands, you sinners, and purify your hearts, you double-minded.

If we are true to Jesus and obey him by faith, we need never be afraid of Satan's power. In the following verses from Romans we are told by Paul that neither life nor death, or any other category of being, in present or in things to come in any remoteness of location space, or any creature or created being, can separate us from God's embrace.

Romans 8:38-39
For I am convinced that neither death nor life, neither angels nor demons, neither the present nor the future, nor any powers, [39] neither height nor depth, nor anything else in all creation, will be able to separate us from the love of God that is in Christ Jesus our Lord.

Romans 10:13
"Everyone who calls on the name of the Lord will be saved."

Faith in God will protect us against any darkness and evil, but I want to now look at how we can be affected in our readings and practice, especially when engaging with spirits. In the gospel of John, Jesus informs Nicodemus that Jesus alone is qualified to teach about salvation. He explains that no earthly teachers can teach you about heaven, because none of them have actually *been* there and come back in physicality with a memory to talk about it. He states that His testimony carries weight because He has resided in heaven and so is the only truly qualified person to tell the truth about salvation.

John 3:13
No one has ever gone into heaven except the one who came from heaven —the Son of Man.

We can determine from this statement that when Jesus uses the term Son of Man He is referring to Himself—after all, He was born of woman. But we are all the Son of Man, and we all indirectly came from heaven, just as God created Adam and Eve. And we know God resides in heaven as Matthew tells us in the very first line of the Lord's Prayer: Our Father Who art in heaven.

In either context, only the Son of Man goes to heaven. The remarkable aspect of this understanding has a profound impact on our interaction with spirits from a psychic perspective because it precludes any other outside influences when trying to communicate with those in heaven. If only Jesus and humans are allowed to reside in heaven, then we cannot be interacting with Satan or any of his minions during our psychic work when talking to the deceased, because Satanic darkness is not present there. Satan and his demons are not the Sons of Men. They were originally created by God as angels and do not have parents. So this verse suggests that angels do not reside in heaven either.

So what can Satan and dark entities do to hamper and influence our work when interacting with those in spirit? They can give us miscommunication and wrong thoughts and ideas. Important messages from your deceased loved ones can be distorted or misheard. This is why it is important to ask questions multiple times to gain clear, definitive answers. Remember, there is the possibility of having an outside influence trick you into mishearing a sentence or word, or making the wrong connections in the deceased's thinking—like a mistuned radio interjecting static or the odd random word.

We have to protect ourselves against such events. This is achieved through prayer, showing humility and asking for God's protection and embrace. The following verses will help you to understand how to protect yourself against these attempts by Satan. We know that God listens and hears all of our prayers, so it is important to undertake them as part of the process of preparation for psychic work and healing. This is reinforced in Psalms.

Psalm 34:17
The righteous cry out, and the Lord hears them; he delivers them from all their troubles.

There is an excellent prayer of protection already written for us in Psalm 91. It is very useful when I undertake paranormal investigation or psychic and healing work. I always take my Bible with me whenever I practice and I have this page marked so I can recite the prayer. I also have a laminated copy of this prayer near me at all times.

Psalm 91:1-16
Those who live in the shelter of the Most High will find rest in the shadow of the Almighty. [2] This I declare about the Lord: He alone is my refuge, my place of safety; he is my God, and I trust him. [3] For he will rescue you from every trap and protect you from deadly disease. [4] He will cover you with his feathers. He will shelter you with his wings. His faithful promises are your armor and protection.

[5] Do not be afraid of the terrors of the night, nor the arrow that flies in the day. [6] Do not dread the disease that stalks in darkness, nor the disaster that strikes at midday. [7] Though a thousand fall at your side, though ten thousand are dying around you, these evils will not touch you. [8] Just open your eyes, and see how the wicked are punished. [9] If you make the Lord your refuge, if you make the Most High your shelter, [10] no evil will conquer you; no plague will come near your home.

[11] For he will order his angels to protect you wherever you go. [12] They will hold you up with their hands so you won't even

hurt your foot on a stone. ¹³ You will trample upon lions and
cobras; you will crush fierce lions and serpents under your
feet! ¹⁴ The Lord says, "I will rescue those who love me. I will
protect those who trust in my name. ¹⁵ When they call on me,
I will answer; I will be with them in trouble. I will rescue and
honor them. ¹⁶ I will reward them with a long life and give
them my salvation."

I like this prayer because it tells us that by faith if we choose
God as our protector we shall find all in him that we need or desire.
Our spiritual life will be protected by Divine grace from the tempta-
tions of Satan. Great security is promised to believers. We have no
reason to fear and whatever happens, nothing shall hurt the believer.
By prayer, we can constantly call upon Him and His promise that He
will deliver us out of trouble. The Lord will manage all our worldly
concerns, and we shall live long enough to do the work we were
sent into this world for until He is ready to bring us into heaven.
Powerful stuff!

I also like to say my own prayers, as they are more personal and
specific to the task I am to undertake. The rules for creating a personal prayer have their formula defined in the Bible, so let us take
our lead from these teachings. Let us study what is explained about
the frame of mind in which our prayers should be offered. It is taken
for granted that all who are Disciples of Christ pray, and if we are
prayerless then we are graceless.

In Matthew we are told that the Scribes and Pharisees were
guilty of two great faults in prayer, vain-glory and vain repetitions.

Matthew 6:7
And when you pray, do not keep on babbling like pagans, for
they think they will be heard because of their many words.

In Ecclesiastes we are told how to address ourselves to the worship of God; by taking time to compose oneself. It is important to
try and stop our thoughts from wandering and focus with meaning
on the right subjects and topics. Many hasty words used in prayer

will appear throwaway and unconsidered and show a lack of respect when in the presence of our Lord.

Ecclesiastes 5:2

Do not be quick with your mouth, do not be hasty in your heart to utter anything before God. God is in heaven and you are on earth, so let your words be few.

The personalized protection aspect of our prayer, to suppress and remove the elements of darkness and evil from the work that we undertake, can be resolved with a prayer like the following:

Dear Lord,

I pray as your humble servant to place a hedge of protection around this room.

Please remove and destroy all forces of darkness and malignance; all spirits, energies and beings of evil that are negative in nature and wish to cause destruction, confusion, pain, anguish, miscommunication, untruths, sorrow and suffering.

Please Lord, leave behind nothing but joy, well-being, success, calmness, warmth and those spirits from the white light that are in your land and embrace.

Please place your hand of protection over the people I am seeing today and myself, so that I may have nothing but pure clear communication without interference. Amen.

I use the process of smudging as I say this prayer. I like to use the Biblically historical frankincense, but you can use incense, sage, smudging wands, candles and other such tools. I walk around the room making sure the smoke penetrates into all the corners, under the chairs and tables, and around the door frames. If you practice regularly in the same room it would be advisable to bless the doors and window frames with anointing oil or holy water. I usually make the sign of the cross with the oil on the lintels above the doors and windows. Do not forget air vents and chimneys and any other places you

believe a dark entity may be able to find a way back in. It is important
to clear the room first with prayer and intensions before you bless anything, otherwise you may be trapping in negative forces that are in the
surroundings and cannot pass beyond the barricade you have created.

The practice of smudging (using dried rolled sage leaves that
are burnt, then blown out to create smoke) was adopted by a number of modern belief systems, including many forms of new age
thinking and eclectic spirituality. It is a method of purifying your
surroundings. While the burning of incense and the use of sacred
fires to produce smoke are found in many cultures worldwide (the
first recorded use of incense was by the Egyptians during the Fifth
Dynasty 2494-2345 B.C.) smudging with sage or other herbs is specifically sacred to indigenous people and represents a different and
culturally-specific practice.

Incense is mentioned 146 times in the Bible and has been employed
in worship by Christians since antiquity. Its practice is rooted in the earlier traditions of Judaism in the time of the Second Jewish Temple. The
smoke of burning incense is interpreted by both the Western Catholic
and Eastern Christian churches as a symbol of the prayer of the faithful
rising to heaven. This symbolism is seen in the Psalm of David.

Psalm 141:1-2
I call to you, Lord, come quickly to me; hear me when I call to
you. 2 May my prayer be set before you like incense; may the
lifting up of my hands be like the evening sacrifice.

The use of incense is actually commanded by God Himself as
outlined to Moses in Exodus.

Exodus 40:26-27
Moses placed the gold altar in the tent of meeting in front of
the curtain 27 and burned fragrant incense on it, as the Lord
commanded him.

In the Revelation of John, incense symbolizes the prayers of the
saints in heaven which infuse upwards towards the altar of God.

Revelation 5:8

And when he had taken it, the four living creatures and the twenty-four elders fell down before the Lamb. Each one had a harp and they were holding golden bowls full of incense, which are the prayers of God's people.

Revelation 8:3

Another angel, who had a golden censer, came and stood at the altar. He was given much incense to offer, with the prayers of all God's people, on the golden altar in front of the throne.

My own personal preference is to use Frankincense. It has a very smoky flame and can be easily blown and maneuvered into corners and under furniture. It has an agreeable perfume and is historic in its Biblical use. Frankincense has been traded on the Arabian Peninsula and in North Africa for more than 5,000 years. It was one of the consecrated incenses described in the Hebrew Bible and Talmud used in Ketoret ceremonies. It was also made as an offering to the infant Jesus as described in Matthew.

Matthew 2:11

On coming to the house, they saw the child with his mother Mary, and they bowed down and worshiped him. Then they opened their treasures and presented him with gifts of gold, frankincense and myrrh.

As well as using incense, I also employ anointing oil for my practices and protection. Anointing oil is mentioned twenty-six times in the Bible and is once again directed to be used by God.

Exodus 35:28

They also brought spices and olive oil for the light and for the anointing oil and for the fragrant incense.

Exodus 30:25
Make these into a sacred anointing oil, a fragrant blend, the work of a perfumer. It will be the sacred anointing oil.

It is important to remember that anointing oil can also be used in healing as well as protection, as outlined in the Prayer of Faith in James.

James 5:13-14
Is anyone among you in trouble? Let them pray. Is anyone happy? Let them sing songs of praise. 14 Is anyone among you sick? Let them call the elders of the church to pray over them and anoint them with oil in the name of the Lord.

You can, of course, have anything blessed. I have blessed many cars in the hope of keeping the occupants safe and clear of danger. The front of the hood makes a wonderful place for a cross to be drawn. I have also blessed jewelry so that the wearer may be protected.

We can also use salt to protect our surroundings and property from darkness and unwanted spirits. The role of salt in the Bible is relevant to understanding Hebrew society during the Old and New Testaments. Salt is a necessity of life and was a mineral crystal that was used since ancient times in many cultures as a seasoning, preservative and disinfectant. It was also utilized as a component of ceremonial offerings and as a unit of exchange. The Bible contains numerous references to salt in various contexts. It is used metaphorically to signify permanence, loyalty, durability, fidelity, usefulness, values and more importantly purification and protection.

The following passages from Leviticus and Ezekiel illustrate the requirement of salt as part of ancient Hebrew religious sacrifices.

Leviticus 2:13
Season all your grain offerings with salt. Do not leave the salt of the covenant of your God out of your grain offerings; add salt to all your offerings.

Ezekiel 43:24

You are to offer them before the Lord, and the priests are to sprinkle salt on them and sacrifice them as a burnt offering to the Lord.

Jesus used salt in a metaphor in the Salt and Light Sermon on the Mount. It is one of Jesus' main teachings on morality and discipleship and outlines his expectations of the people.

Matthew 5:13-16

"You are the salt of the earth. But if the salt loses its saltiness, how can it be made salty again? It is no longer good for anything, except to be thrown out and trampled underfoot."

[14] "You are the light of the world. A town built on a hill cannot be hidden.

[15] Neither do people light a lamp and put it under a bowl. Instead they put it on its stand, and it gives light to everyone in the house.

[16] In the same way, let your light shine before others, that they may see your good deeds and glorify your Father in heaven."

In this passage, Jesus is explaining that the prophets who went before them were the salt of the land of Canaan; but the apostles were the salt of *the whole earth,* for they must *go into all the world to preach the gospel.* It was a discouragement to them that they were so few and so weak, so Jesus is telling them to be as silent as salt and to diffuse like a handful of salt, far and wide, as a small amount goes a long way. The apostles are as good as salt, white and pure, small and diffused like fine grains, useful and necessary. Colossians proceeds to then tell us that we all have this capacity within us.

Colossians 4:6

Let your conversation be always full of grace, seasoned with salt, so that you may know how to answer everyone.

We know that salt represents goodness and purification and is used as a metaphor by Jesus to teach us about our expectations. This makes it a very useful tool when used by a psychic, paranormal investigator or healer. Its indestructible qualities are further highlighted in Numbers.

Numbers 18:19
"Whatever is set aside from the holy offerings the Israelites present to the Lord I give to you and your sons and daughters as your perpetual share. It is an everlasting covenant of salt before the Lord for both you and your offspring."

This everlasting quality is also fused with the ability to repel disease and darkness and to facilitate light and growth.

2 Kings 2:21
Then he went out to the spring and threw the salt into it, saying, "This is what the Lord says: 'I have healed this water. Never again will it cause death or make the land unproductive.'"

I use salt as part of my practice when I am required to clear a property of a negative spirit. It has proved to be very effective to leave bowls of salt around a house where activity is prevalent. For example, if a client feels he is being attacked in his dreams or is experiencing dark energy or spirits in his bedroom, then I would advise him to place a bowl of salt on his bedside cabinet. Salt lamps are also a useful tool and are now widely available.

Recently I was asked to remove a dark energy from a property owned by someone who refused to go into the building based on his experiences. After the property was cleared I walked around the perimeter of the land and placed a circle of salt to stop the entity from returning after I had left.

How do you stop a dark non-human entity from coming back into a building or space? I like to use blessed anointing oil because it has a physical longevity that you can see and an odor that does not just evaporate and disappear in the same way holy water would.

I would work my way around the building making the sign of the cross on door frames, windowsills, fireplaces, air vents and any other ways a dark entity could get back into the property. As I go about undertaking this process I utter a prayer.

Dear Lord,

I humbly pray that you place a hedge of protection around this property,

Please remove all negativity, all spirits or energy of a dark nature,

Any non-human entities that wish to cause evil, negativity, or miscommunication.

Please place your hand of protection over this family and all who reside here,

Bringing peace, harmony, love, comfort, healing and joy.

Amen.

We can ask God to place a hedge of protection around ourselves and any property. This is the armor God provides us with as previously discussed. In the first chapter of Job, God points out to Satan that Job is "blameless and upright, a man who fears God and shuns evil." Satan complains that God has placed a hedge around him and his household and everything he has. Thus proving that Satan cannot access anything that God oversees and protects.

Job 1:8-9

Then the Lord said to Satan, "Have you considered my servant Job? There is no one on earth like him; he is blameless and upright, a man who fears God and shuns evil."

[9] "Does Job fear God for nothing?" Satan replied. [10] "Have you not put a hedge around him and his household and everything he has? You have blessed the work of his hands, so that his flocks and herds are spread throughout the land."

Once protected within a safe environment, I verbalize and state my intent in asking for the things I require for the undertaking of the tasks I wish to achieve (being pro-active in what I wish to come to me).

Be still and know that I am God.

I call upon those working with me from the white light.

I call upon God Almighty, Jesus Christ our Lord, and the Holy Spirit.

I call upon the Archangels Michael and Gabriel, and the angels that are solely the messengers of God.

I call upon my spirit guides and deceased relatives, and the spirit guides and the deceased relatives of the clients I am seeing today.

I am asking you to be with me—I am here ready and willing to receive.

Please clear and cleanse my mind.

Please clear and cleanse my body.

Please clear and cleanse my spirit.

I ask dear Lord that through my lips I may communicate with those that have passed over to your embrace, so that we may find love, happiness, warmth, comfort, peace, guidance, closure, growth, light, harmony, joy, insight and direction.

Amen.

You may, of course, organize your own prayers if you wish. My prayers tend to vary depending on what thoughts come to mind as I recite them. I like to speak them out loud to make sure the intention is firmly placed and without doubt.

Below, I break down my prayer into individual parts and show you the origin of each line. The opening sentence underpins much of what this book is about. It says here I am God—do with me as you will (use me).

Psalm 46:10
He says, "Be still, and know that I am God; I will be exalted among the nations, I will be exalted in the earth."

I then ask for the counsel of the Lord and his son Jesus Christ; I also ask to receive the Holy Spirit.

Acts 1:8
"But you will receive power when the Holy Spirit comes on you; and you will be my witnesses in Jerusalem, and in all Judea and Samaria, and to the ends of the earth."

I then call upon the Archangels Michael and Gabriel and the angels that are solely the messengers of God. I ask for Archangel Michael as the protector and slayer of demons and for Archangel Gabriel for his communication skills. You can also call upon Raphael for his powers of healing. I call upon the angels that work solely with God, making the delineation between the righteous angels and the fallen angels. Remember, Satan and all his demons are angels, too. God's angels guide and protect us. They do not hurt us, play tricks on us, or lie to us. They make formidable allies in our work. God is always watching over us and will appoint angels to guard his children.

Psalm 91:9-11
If you say, "The Lord is my refuge," and you make the Most High your dwelling,[10] no harm will overtake you, no disaster will come near your tent. [11] For he will command his angels concerning you to guard you in all your ways.

Matthew 18:10
"See that you do not despise one of these little ones. For I tell you that their angels in heaven always see the face of my Father in heaven."

It is necessary to learn how to receive. It is of little use *asking* if you are blind to the process of *reaping*, so this aspect of the prayer is important to enforce. We need to be conscious of what we are meant to hear and be heightened in our visual awareness. We are then in a position to undertake the cleansing process for our mind, body and soul.

Psalm 51:2
Wash away all my iniquity and cleanse me from my sin.

Ezekiel 36:25-27
I will sprinkle clean water on you, and you will be clean; I will cleanse you from all your impurities and from all your idols. [26] I will give you a new heart and put a new spirit in you; I will remove from you your heart of stone and give you a heart of flesh. [27] And I will put my Spirit in you and move you to follow my decrees and be careful to keep my laws.

The cleansing process of the mind is very important for me as a clairvoyant because I see pictures presented to me from the spirit world. So I want to be able to distinguish between my own thoughts and those I am being given. I find meditation an important aid to this process. If I clear my mind, then any unconnected random thoughts that enter are not of my own thinking—they are being placed there for my interpretation and knowledge by a third party.

I have shown through the use of the Biblical text that dark and demonic entities will be destroyed and defeated through the practice of good and the faith and love we have in God. What I have progressively discovered over the last several years is that these entities are fully aware that they can be removed and banished, and that I am making my way to their location to do so. Recently a client contacted me in a state of distress. They quite rightly claimed that a dark energy was present in a barn on their property and that they were fearful of entering the building. Upon my arrival I discovered that the barn was very quiet in terms of its paranormal activity and was a very peaceful environment. I did not disbelieve the client, and I have come to understand that the dark energies and non-human beings will vacate a property upon my arrival—not because I hold myself up as a demon-slaying ego-driven individual, but because we are dealing with intelligent beings that realize that to avoid being destroyed or banished it would be advisable for them to just vacate the area until after I have gone. This works great for me, because all I am then required to do is make sure they do not come back in after I have left.

If we have established that most ghosts and spirits are just working or residing in the property, or wishing to get our attention, what do we do next? We must then look to give them the attention they have been striving for. Start by acknowledging them and respond by verbalizing to them that you know they are trying to get your attention and that you will pay more attention. You can ask them out loud if they can help to give you an indication of who they are. This may be as direct as a picture of your grandmother falling off the wall during the course of the next week. Or maybe determining if the activity is centered on a specific date or anniversary that would indicate who the spirit may be. It could just be a feeling you have of who you might believe it to be.

If this concerns you please tell the spirit that you do not wish to be scared and that they are causing you distress. You should find great success in telling the spirit a list of ground rules and reclaiming your own space as your own. There is no reason to be mean, as in respects they actually have a better argument for being in your house than you, especially if they built the property and subsequently resided in it all their life. Most people are reasonable in life and if you wish to be left alone so you can co-habit in the same environment, then that can be very successful. In the house I grew up in we had a ghost that was a previous owner called Herbert, who died in the property. Whenever we saw a shadow move, or a door slam, or the heard the sound of footsteps, we just acknowledged them and shouted out, "Hi, Herbert, how are you?" He never bothered us or caused any problems.

I have found it particularly useful to lay down specific ground rules if you do not wish that spirit to engage or play with your children. Or, for example, if you have to get up early for work the next morning, you may not wish to have any noise past ten o'clock. These are rules that can be verbalized into the space to allow the spirits to listen. I have found this technique to be very affective. People are generally very reasonable and would not wish to cause you or your family distress, even in spirit. Remember that the spirts have a choice and they can, if they wish, create a manufactured reality for themselves in heaven.

There have been instances in my life when demons have been summoned by the practices of those embracing dark magic to confront me. As you would expect, my house is well protected against such conjured creatures. On one occasion I saw the non-human evil entity wandering around my property looking to find a way in through God's protection. On seeing the beast pacing the perimeter, I decided to be proactive in its removal and banishment. I ventured outside to confront the darkness, and on this occasion called upon the help of Archangel Michael. Archangel Michael is mentioned three times in the book of Daniel. The prophet Daniel experiences a vision of Michael after a period of fasting. In the visitation Daniel identifies Archangel Michael as the protector of Israel and refers to Him as a *prince of the first rank* and a protector of the people.

Daniel 10:13-21

"But the prince of the Persian kingdom resisted me twenty-one days. Then Michael, one of the chief princes, came to help me, because I was detained there with the king of Persia.

[14] Now I have come to explain to you what will happen to your people in the future, for the vision concerns a time yet to come."

[15] While he was saying this to me, I bowed with my face toward the ground and was speechless.

[16] Then one who looked like a man[a] touched my lips, and I opened my mouth and began to speak. I said to the one standing before me, "I am overcome with anguish because of the vision, my lord, and I feel very weak.

[17] How can I, your servant, talk with you, my lord? My strength is gone and I can hardly breathe."

[18] Again the one who looked like a man touched me and gave me strength. [19] "Do not be afraid, you who are highly esteemed," he said. "Peace! Be strong now; be strong."

When he spoke to me, I was strengthened and said, "Speak, my lord, since you have given me strength."

[20] So he said, "Do you know why I have come to you? Soon I will return to fight against the prince of Persia, and when I go, the prince of Greece will come;

[21] but first I will tell you what is written in the Book of Truth. No one supports me against them except Michael, your prince."

Later in the vision Daniel is informed about the role of Michael during the *Time of the End* when there will be *distress such as has not happened from the beginning of nations.*

Daniel 12:1
"At that time Michael, the great prince who protects your people, will arise. There will be a time of distress such as has not happened from the beginning of nations until then. But at that time your people—everyone whose name is found written in the book—will be delivered."

In the New Testament Michael leads God's armies against Satan's forces in the book of Revelation, where during the war in heaven he defeats Satan.

Revelation 12:7-9

Then war broke out in heaven. Michael and his angels fought against the dragon, and the dragon and his angels fought back. [8] But he was not strong enough, and they lost their place in heaven. [9] The great dragon was hurled down—that ancient serpent called the devil, or Satan, who leads the whole world astray. He was hurled to the earth, and his angels with him.

Michael and his angels fought against the dragon, and the dragon and his angels fought back. But Satan was not strong enough, and they lost their place in heaven. As Archangel Michael is therefore the protector of people against demons and the wiles of Satan, he is the perfect being to call upon for help through God. His depiction in this role has been a source of creativity for artists throughout the late Renaissance and early Baroque periods of art as depicted perfectly in Guido Reni's Michael in the Santa Maria della Concezione in Rome, 1636.

I prayed for Archangel Michael to come down that night and to wrap his wings around the non-human entity to destroy or banish it in the name of God. It was merely seconds after I had uttered my prayer that I heard the kind of terrible noise only reserved for wild mammals like bears and wolves that have had the misfortune to be caught in an animal trap. It sent a chill through my bones and the hairs stood up on the back of my neck. I will never forget the cries that entity let out as it was being dealt with by the angelic force, and I wish to not experience it again.

In conclusion, there are many tools available for us to use in protecting and banishing darkness. The key is to do everything through God. We have seen that darkness and evil cannot defeat God and the Divine and that in a protected, smudged, blessed room, surrounded by the Holy Trinity and an army of all ranking angels (and with the potential wrath of my deceased grandmother), we should feel secure in the knowledge that Satan will not choose to come near. We can walk through the very gates of Hades without getting scorched. Now we are ready to receive God's wisdom and messages.

Meditation

Meditation is the practice of training your mind to induce a mode of consciousness that creates extended thought, reflection, contemplation and spiritual introspection. It is an important step in preparing us for psychic and healing work. I meditate before I embark on any work I do through God. You may have found yourself doing some of these exercises and activities yourself almost through default—without ever really knowing why—as if the body knows what the spirit requires through the unseen guidance of God's hand.

I have heard many derisions come from all areas of the church around the concept of meditation, so I was actually pleased to learn how many times the word is used in the Bible. The word "meditate" can be found eighteen times, and the word meditation three more. Here are several places where these words are mentioned:

Genesis 24:63
He went out to the field one evening to **meditate**, and as he looked up, he saw camels approaching.

Joshua 1:8
Keep this Book of the Law always on your lips; **meditate** on it day and night, so that you may be careful to do everything written in it. Then you will be prosperous and successful.

Psalm 19:14

May the words of my mouth and the **meditation** of my heart be pleasing in your sight, O Lord, my Rock and my Redeemer.

Psalm 48:9

Within your temple, O God, we **meditate** on your unfailing love.

Psalm 104:34

May my **meditation** be pleasing to him, as I rejoice in the Lord.

Teachings in both the Eastern and Western Christian churches have actually emphasized the use of Christian meditation as an element in increasing one's knowledge of Christ. There have been many prominent proponents of Christian meditation throughout history. St. Ignatius of Loyola (1491-1556) was the founder of the Jesuits; his meditative exercises are still integral to the Novitiate studies of the Jesuit order. St. Teresa of Ávila (1515–1582) believed that no one who was faithful to the practice of meditation could possibly lose their soul. Her writings are seen as fundamental teaching in the area of Christian spirituality. St. Francis de Sales (1567–1622) also introduced new approaches to the processes and techniques for practicing Christian meditation.

We are taught that we are not to abandon God's word, and that God clearly states we can get closer to Him through the process of meditation to improve our knowledge of Him and the things He wants to tell us. This is shown in the following verse from 2 Timothy.

2 Timothy 3:16-17

All scripture is God-breathed and is useful for teaching, rebuking, correcting and training in righteousness, so that the man of God may be thoroughly equipped for every good work.

However we have to be careful how we characterize Christian meditation over meditations that are linked to Eastern practices. There are potential incompatibilities between Christian and non-Christian styles of meditation as the Vatican highlighted in 2003 when addressing New Age thinking. Christian meditation is a process enabling us to become more aware and able to reflect on God's wisdom and words. The Latin translation of the word meditation actually means *to reflect on, to study*, and *to practice*.

Psalm 49:3
My mouth will speak words of wisdom; the **meditation** of my heart will give you understanding.

Meditation can clear the mind of everyday thoughts and clutter so that we can hear the words and messages that are being conveyed. Through meditation we are looking to heighten the personal relationship we have with God and further our understanding. This is especially true when using meditation as a tool to access the spirit realm. David found this to be so, and in Psalm 1 he describes the man who is *blessed* as the man who *meditates*.

Psalm 1:1-2
Blessed is the one who does not walk in step with the wicked or stand in the way that sinners take or sit in the company of mockers, ²but whose delight is in the law of the Lord, and who meditates on his law day and night.

In starting the process of meditation we must learn how to *ground* ourselves. Grounding is the process of staying in the present. It helps to re-orient us back to a sense of the here and now. It also helps alleviate symptoms of dissociation when we experience intense and overwhelming feelings of stress and anxiety. It provides a platform for regaining one's mental focus and helps us connect to both God's energy and the Holy Spirit. I want to assure you through my own practice that meditation can draw you closer to God and heighten your psychic skills.

Everything you have, including your body, came from God. We are all God's creations—the rain, trees, grass, sunshine, mountains, oceans, forests, deserts and animals. So just to feel part of God's creations can be healing and grounding.

Psalm 145:5
They speak of the glorious splendor of your majesty— and I will **meditate** on your wonderful works.

The Bible tells us to meditate on His works and wonders and to be at one with God and nature. I know God exists because I can look out of my window and see a tree. I don't worship the tree, but I appreciate it as the wonder of God's creation. In the same way, I possess rocks and crystals that help me on my spiritual path. They remind me of God's creations. I do not worship the stones and the crystals—this would be in conflict with the Third Commandment, *Thou shalt not make unto thee any graven image*—but all of us can meditate on the wonder of His works.

The first and easiest place to start *grounding* is to take your shoes off and go barefoot. You can be more grounded if you are physically in contact with the ground. And this simple act also serves as a gesture of respect and submission.

Exodus 3:5
"Do not come any closer," God said. "Take off your **sandals**, for the place where you are standing is holy ground."

Joshua 5:15
The commander of the Lord's army replied, "Take off your **sandals**, for the place where you are standing is holy." And Joshua did so.

Isaiah 20:2
At that time the Lord spoke through Isaiah son of Amoz. He said to him, "Take off the sackcloth from your body and the

sandals from your feet." And he did so, going around stripped and barefoot.

The removal of one's sandals or shoes is a custom that has been common in the east since biblical times, especially when entering a temple or somebody's house. One reason is cleanliness, as sandals have dirt and dust on them. More importantly, the reverence of removing one's footwear can be seen in the command given to Moses (and then Joshua) when told they were now on ground rendered holy by the very presence of God. People were commanded to approach God with solemnity and humility. Taking off their sandals expressed an inward reverence through an outward behavior in their worship.

God has a high standard for approaching Him—stringent rules and regulations. For example, in the instructions given to the priests and Levites in the service of the tabernacle, He specifies a lofty standard of propriety. Showing such respect makes it more difficult to be casual, sloppy or rude. It signifies that we have our hearts engaged in our worship and work.

King David learned a hard lesson in disregarding how God's presence was to be approached when he was finally established as king in Jerusalem. In 2 Samuel 6:1-5, David was determined to bring up the Ark of the Covenant; unfortunately, a break in ritual (due to a stumbling ox) saw Uzzah put his hand on the Ark in a steadying action. In an instant, God struck Uzzah dead.

If we are to notice in our inward reflection the subtle messages we receive from the Divine, we must first be free from outside influences or pollution. We must be aware of the chemicals we place in our bodies. That will affect how successful we are at determining those signs and messages. If we are leading a sedentary lifestyle where our minds have become numb and blunt—if we have abused our bodies with poor food choices, alcohol, nicotine, caffeine or other drugs—we will be in a position where a whole army of angels could wander through our lounge and we may never notice them.

Try to introduce more root vegetables into your diet. Produce that comes from the ground is by default grounding.

Proverbs 15:17
Better a small serving of vegetables with love than a fattened calf with hatred.

This statement, written in Biblical times, could easily be applied to our preoccupation with big-corporation, processed, mechanized, fast-food production. So there needs to be an understanding of what kind of foods we are putting into our bodies and what affect they have. The key here is everything in moderation. Although the Bible seems to be neither for nor against alcoholic consumption, it does at times speak very harshly on becoming enslaved to drink or allowing alcohol to control a person, especially to the point of drunkenness. This message can be applied to any other chemical abuses that will influence our thinking or judgment.

1 Samuel 1:14
...and said to her, "How long are you going to stay drunk? Put away your wine."

Isaiah 5:11
Woe to those who rise early in the morning to run after their drinks, who stay up late at night till they are inflamed with wine.

Isaiah 28:7
And these also stagger from wine and reel from beer: Priests and prophets stagger from beer and are befuddled with wine; they reel from beer, they stagger when seeing visions, they stumble when rendering decisions.

Proverbs 20:1
Wine is a mocker, strong drink a brawler, And whoever is intoxicated by it is not wise.

When we are striving to gain knowledge and wisdom from our practices and designs for life, it would be foolish not to acknowledge these areas and be vigilant. Drunkenness also shows a lack of respect for our Lord. It is disrespectful to stand in front of the Lord in a state of inebriation, or under the influence of any other chemical substances. Disrespect, amplified by the influence of alcohol, brought about the death of Aaron's sons who ignored the guidance laid down in Leviticus. Their arrogant and sloppy service, mixed with alcohol for self-aggrandizement, was unacceptable and contemptible to God. The commandment to not drink wine was given to Aaron immediately after his sons' deaths.

Interestingly, when drugs and alcohol un-ground a person, they are more likely to be targeted by dark entities. If you have ever seen a person slumped against a bar on a Friday night, you have probably seen the dark funk that surrounds them. In my experience, ghosts and spirits that were once drug users or alcoholics will be attracted and subsequently attach themselves to individuals who abuse chemicals. Quite understandably, they want to feel the same buzz again of being high or drunk, a physical buzz they no longer receive in spirit.

I was surprised at how many times the Bible actually encourages the practice of meditation through the scripture. If you meditate to gain a closer relationship with God and to clear your mind of outside thoughts, your practice as a psychic and healer will improve. We need to show a love and respect for ourselves as one of God's creations by not over-indulging and abusing our bodies with what we eat and drink. I have been asked many times by individuals who are just starting to access their psychic skills, or are wanting to start on that path, how do I improve, how do I become more psychic? My response has always been, learn to meditate.

Healing

Most of the design and meta-narrative of the New Testament is so intrinsic to the process of healing and saving (emotionally, spiritually and physically) that it's hard to know where to begin. On another level, it appears ridiculous that anyone would admonish a healer as long as the source of healing is not satanic. The practice of removing pain, darkness, illness, negativity and disability from an individual should be universally celebrated and rejoiced. I am aware that healers can be denounced by some elements of our society, and the sad fact is that I have seen people chastised by religious leaders for simply practicing yoga exercises in their own home.

I have been a qualified practicing Reiki healer for many years. I was first introduced to this practice when I met a well-known British psychic and healer during a paranormal event in Derbyshire. She told me that I was a natural healer and volunteered to train me. As a Christian, I was initially concerned about embracing what I then considered to be a Buddhist practice. But further research into the history of Reiki dispelled my fears.

Reiki was developed in 1922 by Japanese Buddhist and Christian, Mikao Usui. It uses the technique of palm healing or hands-on-healing to transfer universal healing energy from the practitioner to the client. Although Usui gained his knowledge of Reiki through the practices of Buddhism, he was inspired to search for wisdom by the story of Jesus Christ, who had healed with the touch of his hand. If I am meditating and praying to God to ask for Him to heal my clients through me, then I believe I am fulfilling what the Bible asks me to do in life.

I have found my healing work to be very beneficial over the years. I have seen cancerous tumors in clients shrink without any scientific reason. I have seen clients rushed to the E.R. with septicemia and then walk away an hour later after defying medical explanation. I have witnessed simple migraines and backaches resolve almost immediately. On one occasion a sweet elderly lady had an appointment to see me and, as she perched herself on my massage table, she unexpectedly removed her prosthetic leg from the knee down. She told me that she needed help with it, implying that she was having issues with her nerve endings. I replied that I was good, but even I would struggle to grow her a new leg.

It is important to realize that we do not have to be practitioners of Reiki to have the ability to heal. The Bible teaches that we all have God in us, thus we can heal in His name. It really is that simple.

1 Corinthians 12:27
Now you are the body of Christ, and each one of you is a part of it.

In the following passage from Corinthians, Paul wrote that believers are ignorant about spiritual gifts. He wanted the people of Corinth to recognize the source of these gifts and why they had been given. By means of rhetorical questions, Paul reminds the Corinthian believers that not all were apostles, not all were prophets, not all were teachers, not all performed deeds of power, not all healed, not all spoke in tongues, and not all translated tongues (languages they had not previously learned). So he was admonishing them to strive for the greater gift, to tell them that they could heal in God's name. He wanted to tell them that they should be striving to embrace the way of love, selfless compassion, care and concern for others. Furthermore, he is stating that those gifts should not be left to wither, but should be put to full use for the benefit of the congregation.

1 Corinthians 12:29-31
Are all apostles? Are all prophets? Are all teachers? Do all work miracles? [30] Do all have gifts of healing? Do all speak in tongues? Do all interpret? [31] Now eagerly desire the greater gifts.

The following statements are directives from Jesus himself and are a clear mandate to go forth and heal in His name. In Matthew, he tells his disciples that all the goods and truths of the church have power from the Lord's Divine Humanity, over all opposing evils and darkness, in order to heal. The word disciple signifies messenger; they were Christ's messengers, sent forth to proclaim His kingdom. Christ gave them power to heal all manner of sickness.

Matthew 10:1
Jesus called his twelve disciples to him and gave them authority to drive out impure spirits and to heal every disease and sickness.

Jesus goes on to say that wherever they go they must proclaim that the kingdom of heaven is at hand. Christ gave power to work miracles for the confirming of this doctrine, and told them that they will receive spiritual gifts through this belief, gaining a communicative spiritual power over all darkness, illness and evil. Healing those that have sick souls.

Matthew 10:7-8
As you go, proclaim this message: "The kingdom of heaven has come near." [8] Heal the sick, raise the dead, cleanse those who have leprosy, drive out demons. Freely you have received; freely give.

We have received, so thus we should freely give. My Reiki master instructed me and gave me attunements for free. I provide free healing for those I know cannot afford my time or simply ask for donations for my practice. Once a week on social media I offer free distant healing for anyone who writes the name of somebody who requires help below my post. This is an important doctrine to follow.

Matthew continues by stating that a soul under Satan's power, and led captive by him, is blind in the things of God. Satan blinds the eyes with disbelief and seals up the lips from prayer. In the conversion of sinners to a life of faith and obedience, the kingdom of God can come unto us. All who do not aid or rejoice in such a change are against Christ.

Matthew 12:28
But if it is by the Spirit of God that I drive out demons, then the kingdom of God has come upon you.

To drive out demons is to heal. To put this statement into Biblical context we must be aware that within Israel there were many lepers (the word leper was also used for any individual suffering a disease that affected the skin or outward appearance). They suffered permanently from their disorders and by the law of the land were deprived of many privileges and advantages, which others enjoyed. It is to cast out the demons (the scourge of mankind) who have taken possession of bodies that the disciples were ordered to do.

Nothing should be more acceptable than to heal sick friends, relations and clients, many of whom have been thought incurable by the science of man. We are clearly given the power to heal, and when we do we confirm the command of Jesus to heal. The good news is that nothing "converts" non-believers more quickly than a healing. What could possibly prove the Divine more than this? It is in every sense hands-on recruitment for Christianity. Remember that with the grace of the gospel there is a salve for every sore, a remedy for every malady. So none should say there is no hope, or that we cannot heal all.

You do not need to be a "qualified healer" (trained in Reiki, for example), although the process of learning to heal always allows you to evolve, grow spiritually, and gain wisdom. We all have God in us, thus we can heal our clients.

Jesus also commanded that we should go forth and bestow the gift of healing upon others. It is His will. He has specifically given man the order to go and perform this process, to heal through Christ.

As healers, we are incumbent to undertake God's directives through Christ. If we fail to deliver healing—if we hold back that gift—it would be in direct conflict to His command.

Stones and Crystals

I use stones and crystals as part of my practice in healing and protection. It is believed they can also bring about a stimulation in spiritual growth and a positive transformation in life experiences. The Bible actually delineates between the use of stones and crystals in two very distinct ways. First, they are written about in terms of their ornamentation, adornment and value in both life and death. Thus their fascinating attraction and value drew the admiration of kings, religious leaders and commoners. In 2 Chronicles we are told that Hezekiah the 13th king of Judah had a great collection of precious stones.

2 Chronicles 32:27
Hezekiah had very great wealth and honor, and he made treasuries for his silver and gold and for his precious stones, spices, shields and all kinds of valuables.

Not only were precious stones valuable, they were also lightweight compared to precious metals and gave a better ease of transport and durability. This also made them the most common bridal gift and dowry in the form of jewelry as described in Isaiah.

Isaiah 61:10
I delight greatly in the Lord; my soul rejoices in my God. For he has clothed me with garments of salvation and arrayed

me in a robe of his righteousness, as a bridegroom adorns his head like a priest, and as a bride adorns herself with her jewels.

Ezekiel tells us that they became a wealthy woman's personal possessions and eventually her inheritance.

Ezekiel 16:11-13

I adorned you with jewelry: I put bracelets on your arms and a necklace around your neck, [12] and I put a ring on your nose, earrings on your ears and a beautiful crown on your head. [13] So you were adorned with gold and silver; your clothes were of fine linen and costly fabric and embroidered cloth. Your food was honey, olive oil and the finest flour. You became very beautiful and rose to be a queen.

It is also documented in a verse from 2 Chronicles that precious stones were also exchanged as gifts between rulers. It is recorded that when the Queen of Sheba visited King Solomon she brought precious stones with her. King Solomon was renowned for amassing a large collection of priceless gems.

2 Chronicles 9:9

Then she gave the king 120 talents of gold, large quantities of spices, and precious stones. There had never been such spices as those the queen of Sheba gave to King Solomon.

As well as a recognition of wealth and their use as decorative adornment and currency, stones and crystals are also used symbolically within the Biblical text and have unique qualities assigned to them. Their value, luminosity and enduring nature make them an appropriate literary image for the glory of the Lord. In the following passage, Ezekiel describes the throne from which God spoke to him. It is adorned with lapis lazuli.

Ezekiel 1:26

Above the vault over their heads was what looked like a throne of lapis lazuli, and high above on the throne was a figure like that of a man.

The link between the glory of God and the qualities associated with stones and crystals explains why Satan adorned himself in them in a bid to compete with that glory.

Ezekiel 28:13

You were in Eden, the garden of God; every precious stone adorned you: carnelian, chrysolite and emerald, topaz, onyx and jasper, lapis lazuli, turquoise and beryl. Your settings and mountings were made of gold; on the day you were created they were prepared.

Be aware that just because Satan adorned himself with precious stones and crystals does not make them evil by association. Remember that angels are also described as having the appearance of crystal. In the following passage, Daniel describes an angel's body as looking like Topaz.

Daniel 10:5-6

I looked up and there before me was a man dressed in linen, with a belt of fine gold from Uphaz around his waist. [6] His body was like topaz, his face like lightning, his eyes like flaming torches, his arms and legs like the gleam of burnished bronze, and his voice like the sound of a multitude.

Topaz is a brilliant crystal that comes in many colors. Daniel would not compare the appearance of an angel to that of a crystal if he believed crystals to be evil.

It is also interesting to note that God actually commands Moses and the Israelites to use all kinds of crystals in Aaron's armor. Here is the perfect example of how a greater value is to be attached to the inherent quality of the precious stones, rather than just for their outward appearance and attraction.

Exodus 39:8-14
They fashioned the breastpiece—the work of a skilled crafts-
man. They made it like the ephod: of gold, and of blue, purple
and scarlet yarn, and of finely twisted linen. ⁹ It was square—a
span long and a span wide—and folded double. ¹⁰ Then they
mounted four rows of precious stones on it. The first row was
carnelian, chrysolite and beryl; ¹¹ the second row was turquoise, lapis lazuli and emerald; ¹² the third row was jacinth,
agate and amethyst; ¹³ the fourth row was topaz, onyx and jasper. They were mounted in gold filigree settings. ¹⁴ There were
twelve stones, one for each of the names of the sons of Israel,
each engraved like a seal with the name of one of the twelve
tribes.

Aaron's breastplate was obviously more than just decorative.
This symbolism is used further when we are told in Revelation
and Isaiah that portions of God's glorious heavenly city, the New
Jerusalem, will be constructed from crystal.

Revelation 21:11
It shone with the glory of God, and its brilliance was like that
of a very precious jewel, like a jasper, clear as crystal.

Revelation 21:18-20
The wall was made of jasper, and the city of pure gold, as pure
as glass. ¹⁹ The foundations of the city walls were decorated
with every kind of precious stone. The first foundation was
jasper, the second sapphire, the third agate, the fourth emerald, ²⁰ the fifth onyx, the sixth ruby, the seventh chrysolite, the
eighth beryl, the ninth topaz, the tenth turquoise, the eleventh
jacinth, and the twelfth amethyst.

Isaiah 54:12
I will make your battlements of rubies, your gates of sparkling
jewels, and all your walls of precious stones.

The text lists twelve layers of precious stones as being the foundations of the spiritual city of the New Jerusalem. There is an opinion that they are the same twelve gems as used in the vestments of Aaron. It is also suggested that the stones are directly connected with each of the twelve Apostles. This then gives rise to the theory that each of the Apostles has been ascribed a specific gem, delineating them with their own importance.

What we must seek to avoid in our work with stones and crystals is the danger of worshipping them over God—worshipping the creation rather than the creator. This concept is highlighted in Micah and Revelation when God utters stern warnings to those who used stones and crystals as symbols of idolatry.

Micah 5:13
I will destroy your idols and your sacred stones from among you; you will no longer bow down to the work of your hands.

Revelation 9:20
The rest of mankind who were not killed by these plagues still did not repent of the work of their hands; they did not stop worshiping demons, and idols of gold, silver, bronze, stone and wood—idols that cannot see or hear or walk.

When using stones and crystals to heal and cure, we must remember that we undertake that practice solely through God.

Psalm 103:2-4
"Praise the Lord, my soul, and forget not all his benefits—

[3] who forgives all your sins and heals all your diseases,

[4] who redeems your life from the pit and crowns you with love and compassion..."

Stones and crystals must only be a tool and a focus to achieve this aim when we are working through God. As I have already described in this book, if we are using the crystals with the intention to do good through God, then we cannot be sinning. Our loving Lord will not punish you for trying to heal your fellow man through His name. We have already seen that He holds a special place in heaven for us, and actually tells us to go forth and undertake this practice.

We are just utilizing the energy and vibrations emanating from the crystals, since God put them there in the first place, in the same way God has provided leaves and grapes for the making of tea and red wine, the health benefits of which are also well documented.

I would now like to look at how crystals are actually made. A crystal is an array of atoms or molecules that are arranged in a geometrically regular shape. Crystals can be formed by one of three basic processes. Firstly, crystals can be created from the processes that take place inside a volcano. These crystals are a product of earth and are therefore part of God's glorious creation.

Genesis 1:1
In the beginning God created the heavens and the earth.

The second way crystals are created is under great pressure. This is how new crystals like topaz and diamonds can be produced. We have already seen that the brilliance of topaz was compared to the body of an angel. Thirdly, the dissolving and recrystallization of minerals can also create crystal formations. Common salt is an example of this process.

Salt has a unique relationship with the psychic and metaphysical world. We have already discussed how it is used as a cleansing tool and can be utilized to prevent paranormal activity. In pagan culture salt is symbolic of the earth element and is a purifier of sacred spaces. As I have already outlined, the Christian faith has embraced many of the practices of pagan religions, and salt is now mandatory in the rite of the Tridentine Mass. It is added to water in the Roman Catholic rite of holy water. Salt is also the third item (which includes an exorcism) of the Celtic Consecration (Gallican rite) that is employed in the consecration of a church.

It would now seem ridiculous to believe that religious leaders would permit the church to use crystals in holy water for blessings, protection and cleansing but would then not allow healing practitioners to use crystals for the same purposes. We must also be aware that modern medicine is already utilizing the qualities of crystals. Science has now realized that diseased tissue has a different vibrational frequency to healthy tissue. It is now possible to stimulate healthy tissue in the same way crystals do, by using vibrational-based therapies like ultrasound and infrared. Medicine, in fact, has been utilizing diamond scalpels in the field of microsurgery ever since the middle of the last century. Modern society in general now uses crystals in almost every type of electronic device, from wristwatches to computers. So are we then to consider that these objects are prohibited to use as some religious leaders and writers would have us believe?

As long as we remember that stones and crystals are just tools to use in the process of healing and medicine, and are not to be given Divine significance, so crystals and rocks must be treated as inanimate objects. But this does not mean they do not carry the powers that are ascribed to them. There are many examples in the Biblical text of Divine energy being given to inanimate objects to cure illnesses and disease. In the following example the objects used were handkerchiefs and aprons. These objects were not worshipped or considered special in their own right, but God endowed them with power.

Acts 19:11-12
God did extraordinary miracles through Paul, [12] so that even handkerchiefs and aprons that had touched him were taken to the sick, and their illnesses were cured and the evil spirits left them.

We have covered that it is acceptable to talk with spirits in the same way Jesus did. If God tells us to use stones and crystals to facilitate God's will, as he instructed Moses when he ordered him to decorate Aaron's breastplate, then there should be no issue. It appears to be a very clear mandate. Thus God should not be displeased if we wear or carry stones and crystals if it helps us to focus our thoughts in prayer and meditation on Him.

Conclusion

Some may say *why bother to even research and write such a book as God is the ultimate judge, so does it really matter*? My hope is that this book will help to inform those who share in the same interests and skills as I do, and perhaps to help others find security and comfort when going about their own work of helping and healing through their gifts. I have seen people suffer public criticism who are blessed with the skills to help others. I know many who harbor fear of being scolded at any moment, so their gifts remain unused (or they covertly practice while enduring the stress of inner conflict). As a historian, author, psychic, healer, paranormal investigator and Christian, my goal was to write a book that removes questioning or fear. If just one psychic or healer reads this book, and it happens to provide the information they need to help their fellow man, then this project has been totally worthwhile.

I also hope this book offers you the chance to question your own thoughts and beliefs, to challenge the often misleading concepts that you have been told, and to compare them to what the Bible actually says regarding psychics, mediums, healers and paranormal investigators. Unfortunately, a change of thinking will not happen in the Christian church overnight—or at all if darkness has its way and prevails in so many areas of life. This would require the majority of Christian society to break from old prejudices and rigid ways of thinking. Leviticus tells us that we should always embrace new ways of thinking and being, with the guidance of the Lord. So we can walk without being ashamed of ignorant, wrong, or biased views placed upon us as practicing psychics, healers and paranormal investigators.

Leviticus 26:13
I am the LORD your God, who brought you out of Egypt so that you would no longer be slaves to the Egyptians; I broke the bars of your yoke and enabled you to walk with heads held high.

Here is a simple list of the main points and themes in this book.

* Do not judge—that is God's job. Just look after your own actions and be true to yourself and your gifts.

Matthew 7:1
Do not judge, or you too will be judged.

* Man is not meant to know what God thinks, so individuals need to stop using God's name to supersede their own thoughts.

Isaiah 55:8
"For my thoughts are not your thoughts, neither are your ways my ways," declares the Lord.

* The Biblical text is telling you to help your fellow man by using your skills; it would be blasphemous not to go forth and heal or talk to the spirits.

1 Corinthians 12:7-11
Now to each one the manifestation of the Spirit is given for the common good. [8] To one there is given through the Spirit a message of wisdom, to another a message of knowledge by means of the same Spirit, [9] to another faith by the same Spirit,

to another gifts of healing by that one Spirit, [10] to another miraculous powers, to another prophecy, to another distinguishing between spirits, to another speaking in different kinds of tongues, and to still another the interpretation of tongues.

- Dark forces will want to see you fail in your work, and those forces will probably falsely claim to be Divine in intention.

2 Corinthians 11:14-15
"And no wonder, for Satan himself masquerades as an angel of light. It is not surprising, then, if his servants masquerade as servants of righteousness. Their end will be what their actions deserve."

- Contradictions will always abound, but gifts bestowed upon us by God should not be questioned. He distributes them to whomever he wishes.

1 Corinthians 12:7-11
All these are the work of one and the same Spirit, and he distributes them to each one, just as he determines.

- From the very lips of Jesus we are told and directed to heal and engage with ghosts. And we are told to heed His every word.

John 14:6
Jesus saith unto him, I am the way, the truth, and the life: no man cometh unto the Father, but by me.

- If you spend a lifetime driving out demons, healing the sick, and delivering freely to those that ask for help (all in God's name), you should not be afraid of being judged.

Psalm 37:4-6
Take delight in the Lord, and he will give you the desire of

your heart. [5] Commit your way to the Lord; trust in him and he will do this: [6] He will make your righteous reward shine like the dawn, your vindication like the noonday sun.

- Embrace the spiritual world if you are a Christian (or religious in any shape or form).

John 4:24
God is spirit, and his worshipers must worship in the Spirit and in truth.

- You can work with and acknowledge the world of spirits and psychic phenomena and still be a Christian. God actually wants you to be aware of this realm.

1 Corinthians 12:1
Now concerning spiritual gifts, brothers, I do not want you to be uninformed.

- Do not follow what others tell you to do, follow your own path and the path God has placed before you by opening your mind to the possibilities.

Romans 12:2
Do not be conformed to this world, but be transformed by the renewal of your mind, that by testing you may discern what is the will of God, what is good and acceptable and perfect.

God has chosen you and wants you to help wrestle and defeat the darkness found residing in the spirit world.

Ephesians 6:12
For we do not wrestle against flesh and blood, but against the rulers, against the authorities, against the cosmic powers over this present darkness, against the spiritual forces of evil in the heavenly places.

We will always meet hypocrites who refuse to read or acknowledge anything written in this book; others will believe that what they
are doing is the Lord's work and see nothing wrong with castigating
and denouncing.

Naysayers should not dissuade you from the path you have been
placed on by God. There will always be individuals that are praying
in church for those parishioners who are sick and in need of healing
but recoil from those who practice healing. There will always be
those that attack and deride the paranormal investigator, even when
the investigator is simply trying to provide evidence that an afterlife
exists.

There will always be individuals who will label all psychics as
satanic but will happily line up and pay to see a modern day "prophet" prognosticating the future, or highlighting those in the congregation who need healing. These are the same members of our community that denounce everything we do as "dark," yet decorate their
yards and lawns in festive Halloween decorations to unwittingly cel-
ebrate the pagan festival of All Hallows Eve (the autumnal equinox
of the Mabon Ingathering—Samhain). Those same individuals may
present righteous behavior, but will utter no derisory comments, or
offer no castigating responses to the action of multi-national grocery
stores that stock little princess Ouija boards on their shelves, complete with decorative pink designs and sparkles.

Ultimately, I will be judged on what I have presented here, and
not a single day has gone by during the writing of this book when
I didn't think: *Am I getting it right? What if I am wrong?* What has
stopped these divisive and unhelpful thoughts (driven by those dark
forces that would not want to see this text published) is the way in
which the Bible clearly outlines every aspect of the themes we have
covered.

Let me finish by asking you to consider the following Bible story that perfectly illustrates why some dark forces appear to affect
some individuals over and over—even if they have had some measure of deliverance. The story also highlights why we should walk
with God at our side.

Matthew 12:43-45
"When an impure spirit comes out of a person, it goes through arid places seeking rest and does not find it. ⁴⁴ Then it says, 'I will return to the house I left.' When it arrives, it finds the house unoccupied, swept clean and put in order. ⁴⁵ Then it goes and takes with it seven other spirits more wicked than itself, and they go in and live there. And the final condition of that person is worse than the first. That is how it will be with this wicked generation."

In simple terms, dark spirits return if they find the house *unoccupied*, the house being a metaphor for a person's body and dwelling (spiritually and physically). The message here is that you have to fill your life with God otherwise Satan will gain a foothold.

Ephesians 4:27
...do not give the devil a foothold.

I Peter 5:8-9
"Be self-controlled and alert. Your enemy the devil prowls around like a roaring lion looking for someone to devour. Resist him, standing firm in the faith, because you know that your brothers throughout the world are undergoing the same kind of sufferings."

Ultimately, we should all walk without fear of darkness, because I have read to the end of the Good Book—and we win!

About the Author

Adrian Lee was born and raised in London, England, before traveling extensively throughout Europe, America and the rest of the world. He graduated from Kent University in 1992 and attended London University from 1996. He studied art history and history methodologies for his master's degree, and more recently religious humanities. He taught for thirteen years in England, becoming the head of several history and art departments and a Local Education Authority Advisor; he currently lectures on all aspects of the paranormal including ghosts, hauntings, UFOs, psychic development and angels.

Lee is the founder of The International Paranormal Society and a member of the Luton Paranormal Society in England. He has comprehensively investigated ghosts and paranormal activity all over the globe. He first became interested in the paranormal after experiencing several events in his childhood home. In his adult life, the idea progressively intrigued him to interface with the dead from an historical perspective. What could be more exciting for a historian than to interview someone who had died two hundred years ago?

Lee first came to Minnesota early in 2008 to work on several paranormal video productions and spent two years working in Minneapolis as the national and international news correspondent for a live paranormal talk radio show on 100.3 KTLK. During this time he also created and worked as the lead writer for a quarterly publication aimed at paranormal investigators. He currently hosts the only weekly paranormal news quiz show, *More Questions than Answers*.

Lee's paranormal investigations are informed by his clairvoyance. He sees detailed pictures in his third eye, presented by the deceased. This allows him to have very precise communication with the spirits. He also has the gifts of remote viewing and clairsentience. During his youth, his psychic sensitivities were dormant for some time; it was through working with other sensitives and being exposed to various kinds of paranormal contact (coupled with his own personal psychic development) that his skills developed to where he can now utilize them freely. Like any other ability, his clairvoyance continues to evolve and is becoming stronger through the implementing of structures surrounding his design for life, critical introspection and practice.

Adrian has also written the books *Mysterious Minnesota: Digging up the Ghostly Past at 13 Haunted Sites*, and *Tales of a Pioneer Town: the Earliest Stories of Sauk Centre, Minnesota*.

Acknowledgements

The following supported me, kept me sane, kept me focused, and were there for me in various ways when I needed them. Without them this book would not have been possible in its current format: Lorna Hunter, Heather Morris, Greg and Kim Gohr, Jyeton Drayna, Kathy Blixrud, Nathan Busch, Terry and Barb Karschnik, Mum, Dad, and Joanne. The rest know who you are.

Made in the USA
Lexington, KY
25 September 2017